NEVILLE COOMER

Sowing the Seed

100 Ways to Preach the Gospel in Five Minutes or Less

Neither do people light a lamp and put it under
a bowl. Instead they put it on its stand, and it
gives light to everyone...

Jesus - Matthew 5:15

Contents

Preface

Over many years, a hundred writers sat at their desks with the same aim – to write a few hundred words that would grab the reader's attention before telling them the Bible's wonderful good news of salvation from the penalty of sin and the certainty of new life with God. What they produced were published as 'tracts' (leaflets) and printed along with many others in their tens of thousands to be distributed on the street or posted through letter boxes. As just one example – since the 1970s until COVID-19 thousands of them were handed out during the annual Edinburgh Festival in Scotland by volunteers from all parts of the UK.

The 100 tracts I referred to earlier have been collated here in this book for two main reasons. Firstly, to keep on 'sowing the seed' – as Jesus explained in the Parable of the Sower (Mark 4:14-20), seed is a picture of the Word of God. In His story, some fell on rocky ground and was removed before germination; some grew for a while and withered due to distracting influences; some fell on good ground and yielded much fruit. Our prayer is that many who need the good news of the Gospel will read this book carefully and their life be transformed to fruitfulness as a result. Secondly, there are many 'seed-sowers' looking for ways to share the good news, and perhaps some of the illustrations used here, along with the key Bible verses and the clear explanation of salvation, will be helpful to you. Please use the material freely. If you would like to obtain printed versions for distribution, many of these leaflets are still available to purchase from Hayes Press (hayespress.org).

Neville Coomer

1

Are You Sure?

- Some people think it'll be enough just to try and live a good life. Maybe you think the same – **but are you sure?**
- Lots of people reckon there's no life after death, so it's not worth thinking about. That may be your view too – **but are you sure?**
- Some even feel that it doesn't really matter what you believe, so long as you are sincere. And you may believe that very sincerely – **but are you sure?**
- Other people have the feeling that it's obvious – going to church and being religious is the answer." You certainly won't be alone if that's what you feel – **but are you sure?**
- Others say there are many different religions and plenty of people are hoping they'll all lead to the same place. This may be what you're hoping too – **but are you sure?**
- It's often said that a God of love won't punish people in hell. You may agree – **but are you sure?**
- Philosophers have said there is no God and you may think they know best – **but are you sure?** Where can we get answers that we can be sure of?

Consider these words from the Bible. This is where you can find out the truth that everyone can rely on:

- "I write these things to you who believed in the name of the Son of God so that you may know you have eternal life" (1 John 5:13).
- "And this is eternal life, that they know you, the only true God, and Jesus Christ whom you have sent" (John 17:3).
- "Whoever believes in the Son has eternal life; whoever does not obey the Son shall not see life, but the wrath of God remains on him. (John 3:36).
- "… if you confess with your mouth that Jesus is Lord and believe in your heart that God raised him from the dead, you will be saved" (Romans 10:9).

Anon.

2

A Matter of Life or Death

Excitement filled the air as throngs gathered near the mighty cataract of Niagara Falls that June day in 1858. Attention was riveted on the 1100-foot tight rope stretched from the American side of the falls to the Canadian side. Charles Blondin, world-renowned tightrope Walker, had just crossed the falls on that rope.

Turning to the sea of watching faces, Blondin spoke. A solemn hush fell over the crowd as they heard his challenge. He wanted to recross the falls with a man on his back! "Do you believe I am able to carry you across?" he asked one in the audience. "I certainly do," replied the man. "Then will you let me do it?" Blondin queried. "Not on your life!" came the quick reply. Turning to another man, Blondin posed the same challenge. "I believe you can carry me across," the man said. "In fact, I have no doubts at all." "Then will you trust me to do it?" the tightrope walker asked. "I will!" the man agreed.

Breathlessly the crowd watched the two men start across the rope. Step after step they moved along. Soon they had reached the centre. The rushing, churning water was unable to erase the sight of the ugly threatening rocks beneath. Slowly but surely, without hesitation, they moved towards the other side. Then they stopped. A guy line had broken, and the rope was swinging dangerously! Blondin spoke in deadly tones to the man on his shoulders:

"You are no longer yourself, Mr Colcord. You are part of me. If I sway, sway with me. Do not try to move or balance on your own, or we will both die. Your complete trust in me is now a matter of life or death." They began moving once more across the wildly swinging rope, and at last they reached the other side. The crowd went wild with relief. Complete trust and obedience of the one man for the other had saved the lives of both.

Another rope has been stretched over a chasm every person must cross. Bridging between time and eternity is the great rope of Christ's salvation. There is only one safe way across this gulf, and that is through complete trust in Him. Sure you've heard this before. Like the first man, you may even believe Jesus Christ is the only way to salvation. But belief is not enough. You must also trust. You may believe without making a commitment. But will you trust? Trust requires action. Make no mistake – salvation is found only in Jesus Christ. Your complete trust in him is a matter of life or death. Delay can be dangerous. **"How shall we escape [judgement] if we neglect so great salvation?" (Hebrews 2:3).** Right now put your trust in Him and commit your life into His hands.

Juleen Turnage

3

Something to Remember!

Remember, remember the 5th of November
Gunpowder, treason and plot.
I see no reason why gunpowder treason
Should ever be forgot...

On 5th November 1605, Guy Fawkes was caught in the cellars of the Houses of Parliament with several dozen barrels of gunpowder. It was the intention of the conspirators to blow up King James I with members of Parliament, and other prominent men of the day. Guy Fawkes was subsequently tried as a traitor with his co-conspirators for plotting against the government. He was a member of an extremist group who thought that Roman Catholics were getting a raw deal from Protestants. Even though some in the government were trying to improve the liberties of Roman Catholics, the group were not prepared to wait for the political process to get what they wanted. They paid a high price for their actions.

The following year, it became an annual custom for the king and Parliament to commission a sermon to commemorate the event. The first of many Gunpowder Plot Sermons was delivered by Bishop Lancelot Andrewes. We all know the children's rhyme, but the annual fixture of 5th November in our national calendar is originally due to the bishop's persuasive sermon in which he reminded people that God is in overall charge of things. His will is done. God had ordained the day in which the King and MPs were saved from death and that Guy Fawkes and his followers were caught.

The sermon was not making a sectarian point, but focused on the need to thank God for his grace in saving us. Andrews based his sermon on words from **Psalm 118:24: "This is the day that the Lord has made; Let us rejoice and be glad in it."** This is something you and I should always remember. Every day we live is a day given to us by God and we should thank him for it. Even when times are bad there is always something for which to thank God. Have you thanked God today? Did you thank him yesterday? Will you thank him when you get out of bed tomorrow? That is something worth remembering to do. But you need to trust Him.

If you put your trust in Jesus Christ, He will save you from something far worse than what threatened King James I. He will save you from God's judgement upon all your sins - your wrongdoing of thought, word, deed. If you put your faith and trust in Jesus Christ, he will forgive you and give you a new life - eternal life. God will not remember your sins – ever.
  Anon.

Tweets, Texts and 5 Words

On Twitter, fans can follow the 'Tweeter' as they describe their daily activity. Millions of messages are sent and received every day. Every topic is covered. Some are about serious world changing events: revolutions, disasters, problems - national news. Others are quite the opposite: fun, frivolous or trivial. Some messages are urgent, immediate, now! Others are almost timeless. Some are global, international, and worldwide. Others are very individual, personal, intimate - speaking about love. The technology is powerful but imposes a 140-character limit. At first this seems restrictive, but even without abbreviation a lot can be said. To follow a Tweeter you have to sign up or search for that Tweeter to find out what they are saying.

What if you wanted to find out what God was saying? And could God's message be squeezed into a tweet? Yes! There's a verse in the Bible that fits into a tweet - it's only 130 characters long: **"For God so loved the world that he gave his only Son [Jesus], that whoever believes in him should not perish but have eternal life" (John 3:16).**

This is a good news message. This is God's message to the world but, most importantly, it's also a very personal message to you! It tells us about God's love. The sender is the God who created the world, and he still loves the world and everything in it. He sent his Son Jesus to earth 2000+ years ago. Jesus lived a perfect life and died a significant death - He chose to die in your place. This makes it possible for you not to "perish" (as the message says) but have eternal life." Radio Scotland has a light-hearted way of getting listeners to tweet them about what they are doing or planning to do. They ask for listeners to use just five words. So people send in "at home with my family" or "on bike ride with children" or "on holiday on the beach." Here's God's message in five words: "God loves you, Christ died." Why not make your response in five words: "Thank you God, I believe..."?

Anon.

5

Feeling the Heat!

The 2022 World Cup football tournament in Qatar took place in November, instead of the usual June fixture dates. This was to avoid the worst of the intense heat of the Middle Eastern desert, where Midsummer temperatures average around 35 degrees C. How would you feel, even just walking for 90 minutes in such a blazing heat, let alone charging around a football field? Even before the tournament, some teams had to spend days training in similar conditions to acclimatise themselves to the dry heat.

Jesus and his followers knew this climate well: they travelled extensively on foot, often in the dry and dusty daytime heat. It's a climate that can easily cause fainting. Anyone without water in the desert - especially if feeling ill - immediately makes finding water the number one priority. One time, Jesus sat by a well at noon, the hottest part of the day. He said to a woman who came to draw water: **"Everyone who drinks of this water will never be thirsty again" (John 4:13)**. Imagine a drink in the desert so thirst-quenchingly effective you'd never need to drink again! You'd be safe, no matter how much of the day's heat you'd face along the way.

At another time, Jesus said: **"Blessed are those who hunger and thirst for righteousness, for they shall be satisfied" (Matthew 5:6)**. He was talking about spiritual thirst and spiritual hunger. The 'water' that Jesus offers is the only thing that can satisfy our need for God's forgiveness. All our best efforts would run dry; unlike a sports team in climate training, we are incapable of adapting to God's standards. If we put our faith in Jesus - his life, death and resurrection - then he promises to make us right with God forever. Jesus said: **"Whoever believes in me, as the scripture has said, 'Out of his heart will flow rivers of living water" (John 7:38).**

Anon.

6

Instant Win?

What amazing ways people use to try to win the Lottery! One man who had an astonishing run of success put all possible numbers in a bucket and drew them out at random. Another, a woman who scooped over £2,000,000 let her little toddler pick the numbers for her. Then there are others who believe that it's the location which counts and then rush to buy their tickets in a "lucky" town. But whatever system is used the fact has to be faced that the majority of people who do the lottery end up disappointed. Most are eternal optimists, however, and even after a run of failures feel sure that one of these days they're going to strike it rich.

If you are on the lottery trail, ask yourself the question, "What would I do with it if I had a really big win?" Maybe you already have. You've already fantasised about a new house, a posh car, holidays abroad, and giving up your job. But the one thing you will not be able to buy, however much you win, is *happiness*. In fact it might just be possible you'll be far less happy than when you started. Why should this be? Here's what Jesus Christ said, **"A man's life does not consist in the abundance of all his possessions" (Luke 12:15).** This is why Jesus threw out the challenge - a challenge which is still relevant today - **"What good will it be for a man if he gains the whole world yet forfeits his soul?" (Matthew 16:2).**

Let's remember that thought that what we surround ourselves with now will all be left behind one day. As the Bible puts it, **"Naked a man comes from his mother's womb, and as he comes, so he departs" (Ecclesiastes 5:15).** But the one thing which is going to last is your never-dying soul. God wants you to spend eternity with him - that's true *happiness*. As the psalm put's it, **"You will fill me with joy in your presence, with eternal pleasures at your right hand" (Psalm 16:11).**

To ensure this could be so, **"God ... gave His only begotten Son, that whosoever believes in Him should not perish but have everlasting life" (John 3:16).** Are you looking for happiness? You have just read God's Word telling you where it can be found - now you can make it your very own.
  Archie Hall

7

You Didn't Tell Me!

Whether it was a dream, or my waking thoughts one morning I cannot say; but the picture remains, along with the phrase: you didn't tell ME!! The vivid scene was of Judgement Day and someone pointing the accusing finger at me: someone with whom I talked the business of this world but failed to talk the business of the world to come! I can hear the words now:

- "You didn't tell ME - I was a Sinner!"
- "You didn't tell ME - I couldn't save myself from sin!"
- "You didn't tell ME - I need to have a Saviour."
- "You didn't tell ME – God so loved ME - a sinner!"
- "You didn't tell ME - How to receive this Eternal Life."

Although you may not be the one in the writer's dream, you have received this and you are reading in it what is called God's "Day of Grace." This is your day of opportunity to hear - and mine to talk to you frankly -about *Eternal* business. **"Another day is coming too" (Acts 17:31)** - called God's "Day of Judgement" it hasn't arrived yet - what a mercy! So NOW...

- I want to tell **YOU** - that the Word of God, the Bible, says you and I are sinners: **"All have sinned and come short of the glory of God" (Romans 3:23).**

- I want to tell **YOU** - that you cannot save yourself and I cannot save myself. The Bible says, **"All our righteousnesses are as filthy rags"** (Isaiah 64:6).
- I want to tell **YOU** - that you and I both need a Saviour, and this is God's son, the Lord Jesus Christ **(Acts 4:12).**
- I want to tell **YOU** - that God loves sinners: loves you; loves me! **"God commends his love towards us, in that, while we were yet _sinners_, Christ died for us" (Romans 5:8).**
- I want to tell **YOU** - that you can receive Eternal Life through God the Son **(John 5:24).**

"BUT HOW?" you ask. Acknowledge before God that you are a sinner, repent of your sin, and believe that the Lord Jesus Christ came from heaven and died for you on the Cross of Calvary as your sin-bearer; that He rose again from the dead, and is living today. Accept by faith this same Lord Jesus as your living Saviour and ask him to come into your heart in life, trust him to keep you and help you confess Him before others.

Anon.

8

What Is Life?

Life is a 'giggle' says the teenager; a 'grind' says the man at the workbench; a 'booze-up' says a man in the pub; 'a rat race' says a business executive; a 'scrounge' says a tramp; a 'struggle' says a widow surrounded by children; a 'moan' says the man on the dole; a 'groan' says a sick man. "A mist" says God (James 4:14), for no matter how long you may live, in God's eyes your life is so short that it is just like a mist. Some mists last longer than others, but all are transient. Because of the brevity and uncertainty of life, it is important that we don't fritter it away. Once you leave this life, opportunity will be gone forever. As the Bible says, **"It is appointed for man to die once and after that comes judgement" (Hebrews 9:27).** It is essential that you grasp the opportunity which life alone gives of getting into the right relationship with God. This can come only in one way - through his Son Jesus Christ who said: **"I am the Way, the Truth and the Life; no man comes to the Father, but by Me" (John 14:6).** If you have never received Jesus Christ, you have never yet experienced "Life" with the capital "L". There is a wonderfully thrilling experience awaiting once you do, for He alone can lead you from doubt and fear into glorious certainty, from constant defeat through indwelling sin to victorious living. This then is your moment of decision: what is your life going to be from now on? A caricature of what life is meant to be? Or allow for a life of power and prospect through Jesus Christ? Only you can decide.

Anon.

9

Good News in 30 Seconds

In an age of sound bites, is it possible to summarise in 30 seconds what God wants to say to us? A story is told of a child in Martin Luther's time who only thought about God with dread and as a terrible judge. In the stern house where she grew up, this was the only way God was presented to her. She never heard about God's gentleness or his affection. But one day in her father's printing office, she picked up a scrap of paper, and found written on these words: **"For God so loved the world that he gave ..."**

These were the only words that were on the piece of paper, but even this little fragment was a revelation to her. God loved! Loved the world - and loved it well enough to *give* something! She didn't know what He gave, but it was enough for her to know that God loved as much as that. This new thought changed her view of God. What a comfort to her now to think of God as one who loved her. She only had a part - but we have the complete verse!

"For God so loved the world that he gave his only Son, that whoever believes in him shall not perish but have eternal life."

This verse contains the best news ever in even less than 30 seconds! But let's take a closer look. You find this verse in the New Testament of the Bible. It's John chapter 3 verse 16.

- **"For God …"** – this shows us the source of this gift that's on offer. It begins with God – not us.
- **"… so loved the world …"** – this shows us the depth of God's divine love. "not that we loved God, but He loved us …" (1 John 4:10).
- **"… that he gave …"** is the measurement – what His love prompted him to do; How far He would go.
- **"… His one and only Son …"** the Lord Jesus Christ. In giving up his own Son there must be an important *purpose* for doing this.
- **"… that whoever believes …"** – what God is offering you here and now is available to everybody – but it's only given to be received by those who believe. You cannot work or pay for this – it's all been done by the sacrifice of the Lord Jesus on the cross.
- **"… shall not perish…"** This indicates an escape from perishing or dying. God's justice says we certainly deserved to die. When God says, "do this" we say, "I will not." and when he says, "don't do this" we say, "I will." However, because God's punishment for this disobedience fell on Jesus instead of you and me, we can escape what we rightly deserve!
- **"… but have eternal life"** – it's the free gift of God. *Take it!* You can't get it any other way than by simply believing.

David Richardson

10

What Can Money Buy?

Money can buy… a bed *but not* sleep; books *but not* brains; food *but not* appetite; finery *but not* beauty; a house *but not* a home; medicine *but not* health; luxuries *but not* culture; amusements *but not* happiness; a cross *but not* a saviour; a church pew *but not* heaven. What you cannot buy you can have as a gift: **"The gift of God is eternal life through Jesus Christ our Lord" (Romans 6:23).** God invites you to come and receive it: **"Come, all you who are thirsty, come to the waters; and you who have no money, come, buy and eat! Come, buy wine and milk without money. And without cost" (Isaiah 55:1).** What will happen if you ignore this gift? All the money in the world will not be enough to buy you out of hell if you do not accept the salvation that Christ offers you. **"Seek first the Kingdom of God … and all of these things will be given to you as well" (Matthew 6:33).**

Anon.

11

Penalty Missed

The FIFA World Cup final - so much at stake! For the winners it's glory, worldwide fame and that beautiful golden trophy; for the losers, the agony of defeat. Football can be a very cruel game. In the 1994 final, all eyes were on the Italian striker Roberto Baggio. Italy and Brazil had drawn one-all in normal time and extra time failed to break the deadlock. So it came down to penalties and sudden death. Baggio had to score. He missed. Brazil were the winners.

So much to win, yet so much to lose in just a few seconds! Bill Shankly, the legendary Liverpool manager, once said: "Some people think football is a matter of life and death. I can assure them it is much more serious than that" (Sunday Times, October 4, 1981). Baggio would probably have agreed. Jesus said, **"What will it profit a man if he gains the whole world, and loses his own soul? (Mark 8:36).** What did Jesus mean? Hard as some might find it to believe, there *are* more important things in life. Our soul is what makes us who we are; the Bible says we will either live forever or be lost forever. So losing in the final of the World Cup suddenly seems insignificant by comparison!

The Bible tells us that the wrong that is within us (our sin) carries a clear penalty - a consequence. It prevents us approaching a holy God and having the relationship with Him that we were created for. Ultimately, the result of sin will be that we forfeit heaven, and the possibility of us enjoying the love of God will be lost forever. That's such a serious thing that the Bible describes it as death (Romans 6:33).

Thankfully, there is good news. Despite what we are by nature, God loves us. He gave His own son, Jesus, to die as a substitute for us so that we missed the penalty of sin forever. If we really believe this in our hearts and thank God for it, we will be saved - saved to know God as our Father and Friend, and guaranteed to be with Him forever once our life here is over (John 3:16). So much to be lost, but so much to be won in just a few seconds. Make sure you do not lose your soul. Make the right choice today: **"Believe on the Lord Jesus Christ, and you will be saved" (Acts 16:31)**. It really *is* a matter of life and death!

Martin Jones

12

Imagine

There is a John Lennon memorial paving in Central Park, not too far from the place where he lost his life. One of his songs says: **"Imagine there's no heaven ... no hell below us ... nothing to kill or die for ... no religion too ... imagine all the people, sharing all the world ..."** These words are based on two common assumptions: 1. That there is no afterlife and 2. That people are essentially good. Many people imagine just as John did, that if only we can overcome religious and cultural prejudices, we'll all live together in peace!

Sadly, the truth from God's word, the Bible is very different: **"There is no one righteous, no not one ... and the way of peace they do not know" (Romans 3:10,17).** In 1864, Robert Annan, a lay preacher in Dundee, jumped into the river Tay to save a drowning man. Tragically, Robert himself was drowned. No one knew why, but when leaving home that day, he'd used some chalk to write 2 words: On the gate he wrote "death" and on the pavement he wrote "eternity." He left behind a powerful reminder that death is not the end with nothing beyond. It opens into eternity and **"... man is destined to die once, and after that to face judgement" (Hebrews 9:27).**

The Bible informs us that Adam and Eve, our first parents, disobeyed God. From Adam we inherit our selfish, rebellious nature, the root cause of human misery. **"Therefore, just as sin entered the world through one man, and**

death through sin, in this way death came to all men, because all have sinned" (Romans 5:12). Like Robert Allen who gave his life for a drowning man, so Jesus Christ came from heaven and gave his life for us on the cross. **"For scarcely for a righteous man will one die ... but God demonstrates His own love toward us, in that while we were still sinners, Christ died for us" (Romans 5:7,8).** He overcame death for us and rose again, so whoever accepts him as their Saviour has their sins forgiven by God and receives eternal life.

This is too important an issue to leave to your imagination. Robert Annan accepted Jesus as his Saviour. Have you?

Anon.

13

Trapped!

In October 2010 worldwide TV news channels broadcast live pictures of the dramatic rescue of 33 miners in Chile, trapped for 69 days, 700 metres (2041 feet) below the surface of the earth. The extensive operation involved drilling through hundreds of metres of solid rock to save them. There were emotional scenes as one by one, each miner was reunited with his family on the surface. One knelt and offered a prayer of thanksgiving to God. How grateful the miners were to all these engineers and workers who worked tirelessly to rescue them. As the world watched, no one questioned the multi-million dollar cost of the massive operation. The lives of 33 men were at stake: who could place a value on that? Nearly 2000 years ago, on a hill called Golgotha outside Jerusalem, God valued your life and mine so highly that he mounted a rescue operation far more significant and far more costly than any human rescue before or since. On the cross, the Son of God died bearing our sins so that we could be forgiven and have eternal life. God sacrificed his beloved Son to rescue you from a lost eternity in Hell. The Bible says that whoever believes on Jesus will not perish but have everlasting life (see John 3:16). The miners would have been foolish to turn their backs on the rescuers. Will you walk away from God's rescue plan? Or will you say from your heart: "Thank you Lord Jesus for dying on the cross to save a Sinner like me"?

Anon.

14

Three Basic Problems

We all know how the world has radically changed. Just in the last decade we have seen dramatic advances. But with all our progress three basic problems remain. They have plagued the human race during thousands of years of history.

- **Sin** has not changed. We have changed its name. We've tried to clean up the old, depraved nature of man. But men are still sinners, and the results of sin are still disease, disappointment, despair, disillusionment and Hell.
- **Sorrow** has not changed. Sorrow is still the universal language of the world today. The great tragedies appear on the front of pages of our newspapers but there is also that personal, crushing sorrow that comes to individuals.
- **Death** has not changed. We will try to change its appearance. We place the body in a beautiful coffin and dress up the funeral with flowers. But regardless of what we call death or how we may address it up, death is real, hard and cruel.

These three problems make up a man's history. His past is filled with sin; his present with sorrow and certainty of death faces him in the future. To the average man it can all seem rather hopeless when he thinks about it. However, it has been proved millions of times over that Jesus Christ can meet and solve these three basic problems in your life. There is a verse in the Bible which reads: **"Jesus Christ the same yesterday, and today, and forever" (Hebrews 13:8).**

- **"Yesterday"** – the past, when He was on earth He made atonement, atonement for your sin, for your past.
- **"Today"** – now, in heaven, He is an advocate, interceding for those who place their trust in Him.
- **"Forever"** – in the future, He will return to be King of Kings and Lord of Lords.

As Saviour, He can settle your sin problem. Right now He can meet your every need and lift every burden. As the coming Sovereign King, He can give you hope. Let Him deliver you from the penalty of past sin. Let him deliver you from the perils of the present trouble. Let him deliver you from the fear of the future. **"Whoever shall call upon the name of the Lord shall be saved" (Romans 10:13).**

Anon.

15

Pick 'n' Mix

What's so attractive about the pick 'n' mix stand in shops? For me, it's because you can get a bag full of all your favourite sweets and leave behind the ones you don't like - rejecting the green wine gums and choosing all the reds you could possibly want! If only life was like that. Wouldn't it be great if we could experience all the best bits and avoid the difficult, challenging and painful situations? But life isn't like that. Life seems rather to give us a bag that's full of sweet and sour experiences.

So, how do we navigate this mixed-up life, and make sense of the world around us? Consciously, and often subconsciously, we allow ourselves to be influenced by people who seemed to us to have good advice and perspectives. So we might look for the founders of the world religions for guidance, absorb the philosophies of inspirational thinkers and leaders, and follow the advice of gurus and celebrities. It's a pick 'n' mix approach as we search for truth and life. But where does it really help us understand where we've come from, where we going to and what's happening around us just now?

The Christian faith is unique. The Bible isn't simply good advice written by people like us, it's actually God's revelation of himself to us, if we pick certain aspects of Christianity and reject others, we're missing out on a personal relationship with God himself. Jesus Christ, God's eternal Son, made this bold statement: **"I am the way and the truth and the life" (John 14:6).** When he said, "I am the way," he was claiming to be the only way. When he claimed, "I am the truth," he was stating that nothing else is the truth. And when he said, "I am the life," he was saying that it is only through him that we can have life - now and in the future.

Christianity is not a belief system; it's not just another religion amongst the other world faiths; it's fundamentally about a relationship with God through Jesus Christ: **"To all who received him, to those who believed in his name, he gave the right to become children of God" (John 1:12).**

Will you take the time to consider Jesus claims today?
  Anon.

16

Claim Your Rights!

Have you claimed all your rights? It was recently reported that more than £16 billion in means-tested benefits and tax credits currently goes unclaimed every year in the UK! It is remarkable that such available provision goes unclaimed year after year! 27 leading charities have called on the government to set targets to improve take up of welfare benefits and tax credits, highlighting the desperate need of those in poverty. Spearheaded by the Citizens Advice Bureau, they have written to the Secretary of State for Work and Pensions asking that more be done to ensure that the money earmarked for those in the greatest need reaches them.

These are not the only rights that go unclaimed; in fact, there is one right available to everybody which many people just don't even know exists! When Jesus died on the cross for the sins of the whole world, God his father made available a right which anyone can claim: **"To all who receive him, to those who believe in his name, he gave the right to become children of God" (John 1:12).**

This right is not automatically given at birth or by a childhood ritual. It is only given to those who will claim it by believing in Jesus who took the punishment for all our sins. He died in our place on the cross. This spiritual benefit is not means-tested. It doesn't matter how few or how many sins you have because:

"There is no difference, for all have sinned and fall short of the glory of God, and are justified freely by his grace through the redemption that came by Jesus Christ" (Romans 3:22-24).

If you believe with all your heart that Jesus died for you, then you become his forever: **"I know them, and they follow me. I give them eternal life, and they shall never perish; No one can snatch them out of my hand. My Father, who has given them to me, is greater than all; No one can snatch them out of my Father's hand" (John 10:27-29).**

Please claim this benefit today!
   Steve Henderson

17

Questions

The boy's mother was becoming frustrated as he led her from one cage to another. There were always so many questions you could ask at the zoo.

"What does this animal eat?"... "I don't really know"
"Where does this one come from?"... "I'm not quite sure"
"How old do you think it is?"... "it's difficult to tell"

And so it went on until he asked, "Do you mind me asking all these questions?" "Oh no," his mother replied, "If you don't ask, you'll never learn anything." People nearby who had heard part of the conversation smiled despite all his questions. The boy had, in fact, learned nothing!

It's not only children who like to ask questions. TV quiz games are popular with all ages. Of course, some questions are harder than others. Some are about matters of fact which we either know or don't know; others raise much deeper issues. Take, for example, a question asked by a deep thinker who lived early in human history, who asked about man and God, **"But how can a mortal be righteous before God?" (Job 9:2)**. Or, to put it in other words, how can we be in the clear before God who is our judge?

The question reveals our problem - we've all fallen short of God's perfect standard. We have missed the mark; we are all sinners. This shows up in society at large and in our own lives. We may be good at hiding our wrongdoing, but we still have thoughts which are often unkind and unclean. We talk of turning over a new leaf but we're only kidding ourselves. As the leopard cannot change its spots, neither can we change our tendency to do wrong. And we certainly cannot make up for past wrongs in God's sight.

How then can God accept us as being without fault? There is only one solution, one which God offers us in Jesus Christ, his Son. In his life here on earth Jesus provided the answer to our question when he taught: **"Whoever believes in the Son has eternal life, but whoever rejects the Son will not see life, for God's wrath remains on him" (John 3:36).**

When dying on the cross Jesus was punished for our sins that we might be accepted by God. When we ask forgiveness from God and thank Him that Jesus Christ died for us, God grants forgiveness and assures us of eternal life. **"... God demonstrates His own love for us in this: While we were still sinners, Christ died for us" (Romans 5:8).**

Brian Johnston

18

Too Busy?

He was quite an ordinary man sitting on a train with his nose buried in a paper. Suddenly as the train was leaving a station, he looked up with dismay on his face as uncertain what to do next. He shot forward to the edge of his seat, then realising that there was nothing he could do, he quietly folded his paper and sat back. To anyone watching the drama it was obvious what had happened; he had missed his station. Why? He had been too busy with what he had been doing to think of where he was going.

And of course he is not alone; there are millions in the world who are the same. Business executives caught up in the rat race: people engrossed with the daily round of bringing up a family: students immersed in studies and the shaping of a career, all these, and many more, are running the same risk – they are too busy with what they are doing to think of where they're going. Doubtless they intend to think out this whole question of life, its meaning and what follows. But the years slip by, and this year finds them no better prepared than they were last year.

Are you like that? Are there things that so absorb you that you're letting these weighty considerations have second place or even no place at all? If so, listen to this most searching of all questions: **"What shall it profit a man, if he shall gain the whole world, and lose his own soul?"** (Mark 8:36).

Nothing material, nor any achievement, can ever compensate you for the loss of this most precious of all possessions, your soul. To find yourself in eternity unprepared will cause not just a moment's dismay but an endless remorse. It is the supreme disaster. Far better than to have the matter settled here and now God says, **"I have set before you life and death ... therefore choose life" (Deuteronomy 30:19).** The way of life is embodied in the acceptance of a person, Jesus Christ, who said, **"I am the Way the Truth, and the Life" (John 14:6).** When will you accept him?

Archie

19

No Time for God

"I've no time for God!" The speaker was a young man. He was tinkering around with his old sports car when I handed him a gospel leaflet. Further up the road I met an elderly gentleman, kindly and polite, and his comment was, "I'm not sure that there is a God at all." Youth and age were saying the same thing, in effect, that their lives were so busy that they had shut out God. Youth, middle age, old age—it is the same tale. In all walks of life, folks are filling their lives with so many things that they find no time for God. No time for God! It's an alarming thought, really. What if the tables were turned and God had no time for us! Have you ever contemplated that? Paul, the great preacher of the first century, said: **"The living God, which made heaven, and earth, and the sea ... did good, and gave us rain from heaven, and fruitful seasons, filling our hearts with food and gladness"** (Acts 17:24).

If God forgot us there would be no food on our tables! More serious still, there would be no breath in our bodies, for the same preacher said: **"The Lord of heaven and earth ... giveth to all life, and breath, and all things"** (Acts 17:24-25). He gives to all—the young man with his sports car, my old friend with his set ideas, and you, whoever you are. Whether you think about God or not, He feeds you, clothes you, and daily showers you with many gifts, not the least of which are life and breath. Eighteen times per minute each one of us breathes; 1,080 times per hour and 25,920 times per day–every breath from God's good hand. How many days go by without us giving a thought for the great Giver?

No time for God! The Bible tells us of a farmer who was so busy making money that he left God out of his reckoning. He conveniently forgot that it was God Who made His harvest grow. When he had gathered what he thought was sufficient to give himself a good time, God spoke to him and said, **"Thou fool, this night thy soul shall be required of thee; then whose shall those things be, which thou hast provided?" (Luke 12:20)**. One day you and I also shall draw our last breath, and then we shall meet God who all our life long has provided so many daily gifts. No time for God? Be wise and take time as you read this message to think of the kindness of God to you. If you live without God you will die without God and that would be to die without hope. But there is no need for such a tragedy, for "the kindness and love of God our Saviour toward man" has been for ever demonstrated at Calvary. God loves you and the great proof of His love is that He gave His Son to die for you:

> **"God commendeth His love toward us, in that, while we were yet sinners, Christ died for us" (Romans 5:8).**

> **"God commandeth all men everywhere to repent because he hath appointed a day, in the which he will judge the world in righteousness by that man whom he hath ordained" (Acts 17:30,31).**

We are sinners, all of us, and our sins deserve eternal death, but Christ has died to save us. God calls upon us to acknowledge our sin against Him, to repent of it, and then receive His Son as our Saviour, committing our lives to Him. God waits for this response from your heart to His great giving. Will you not respond today?

Alan Toms

20

Special Offer

We are fast becoming a nation of "special offer" hunters. Who doesn't enjoy buying things at cheaper prices? We all like to believe we're getting a bargain! Many people can hardly believe it when they hear that God has been making a "special offer" for centuries - and that his offer is open to everyone, everywhere. They want to know what the catch is! But it's a fact -he's making his "special offer" to you right now! Many people know that Jesus Christ died on the cross but forget that the world is made up of countries, cities, towns, villages, and families - and *individuals* like you and me. The Bible - the Word of the Living God - says that **"sin separates from God"(Isaiah 59:2).** This is quite reasonable. God's perfect and holy character stands in complete contrast to the thoughts and motives of our hearts. The Bible is right when it declares **"All have sinned" (Romans 3:23).** We have all fallen short of God's standard. But God's "Special Offer" is this: **"While we were still sinners, Christ died for us" (Romans 5:8).** We don't have to wait until we are perfect before we can receive his offer. We can receive complete forgiveness for sins now and accept his free gift of everlasting life. But how? Jesus said, **"No man comes to the Father but by me" (John 14:6).** Will you accept this fact that He died for your sins **"according to the Scriptures"? (1 Corinthians 15:3).** Salvation is your free pass and pardon. The full price of this blessing has already been met by Jesus Christ. It is God's "Special Offer" to you today.
  Keith Nolan

21

God Answers

Have you ever wished you could God ask a question? Here are some questions you may have thought about - with answers straight from the word of God - the Bible.

1. **Am I accountable to God?** Yes, each of us will give an account of himself to God. (Romans 14:12) Does God see all my actions? He knows about everyone, everywhere. Everything about us is bare and wide open to the all-seeing eyes of our living God; nothing can be hidden from him to whom we must explain all we have done (Hebrews 14:13).
2. **Does he charge me with sin?** If we could be saved by His laws, then God would not have had to give us a different way to get out of the grip of sin - for the Scriptures insists we are all its prisoners. The only way out is through faith in Jesus Christ; the way of escape is open to all who believe in him (Galatians 3:22).
3. **Will he punish sin?** It is for a man's own sins that he will die (Ezekiel 18:4). For the wages of sin is death (Romans 6:23).
4. **Must I die?** He is not willing that any should perish, and he is giving more time for sinners to repent (1 Peter 3:9).
5. **How can I escape?** Believe on the Lord Jesus and you will be saved (Acts 16:31).
6. **Is He able to save me?** He is able to save completely all who come to God

through him (Hebrews 7:25).

7. **Is He willing?** Christ Jesus came into the world to save sinners (1 Timothy 1:15).

8. **Am I safe by believing?** All who trust him to save them have eternal life (John 3:36).

9. **Can I be saved right now?** Right now God is ready to welcome you. Today he is ready to save you (2 Corinthians 6:2).

10. **As I am?** Some will come to me, and I will never, never reject them (John 6:37).

11. **Will I fall back again?** And he is able to keep you from slipping and falling away (Jude 1:24).

12. **When saved, how should I live?** He died for all, so that all who live might no longer live for themselves, to please themselves, but to spend their lives pleasing Christ who died and rose again for them (2 Corinthians 5:15).

13. **What about death and eternity?** I am going to prepare a place for you. When everything is ready, then I will come and get you, so that you can always be with me where I am (John 14:2).

Anon.

22

A Pocketful of Posies

"Ring a ring of roses, a pocketful of poses, A-tish-oo! A-tish-oo! We all fall down!" In the school playground, or in the garden at home, we danced in a circle reciting these words until we collapsed on the ground yelling "all fall *down!*" What fun we had! But there's a sad story behind this children's rhyme. The rhyme takes us to the quiet English village of Eyam in the year 1665. The village tailor had just received a box of cloth by waggon from London. Within two days he was killed - struck down by a fever with red rashes on his body. This was the sign of the killer disease. It is remembered in the rhyme - "ring a ring of roses."

The villagers were terrified. They recognised that this was the plague that decimated London's population. It must have been brought in by infected fleas in the cloth that the tailor had received from London. Various medicines were tried. "A pocketful of posies" recalls how people carried bunches of flowers in the hope that this would protect them. To stop the spread of the plague, the people of Eyam agreed on a heroic act of self-sacrifice: to completely shut themselves up with the plague. Many of them realised this would be a death sentence. Nevertheless, a stone circle was put around the village to mark the boundary. Food had to be left there, and money to pay was left in running water. But the time it had run its course the plague had claimed 260 of the 350 inhabitants.

That sacrifice is an incredible example of human love. They died so the others could live. **"Greater love has no man than this, that he laid down his life for his friends" (John 15:13).** These are the words of Jesus Christ. Today, people are still moved by an act of supreme love. Jesus himself, laid down his life to save us from the plague of sin that is a raging infection through all human nature: Sin spoils lives. It exploits the weak and it wrenches families apart. Sin separates us from God. But the power of sin is broken when we believe that Jesus was crucified and died for our sins:

- **"God demonstrates his own love for us in this: While we were still sinners, Christ died for us" (Romans 5:8).**
- **"This is how we know what love is; Jesus Christ laid down his life for us" (1 John 3:16).**
- **"Believe in the Lord Jesus, and you be saved" (Acts 16:31).**

Brian Johnston

23

Nobody Is NOT Loved

Many people don't like themselves. They can have lots going for them and be highly respected by others, but then they look at themselves - and hate what they see. Is this you? What destroyed yourself esteem? Bullied at school? Failed exams? Business 'gone to the wall'? A failed relationship? No? Perhaps your life has been quite uneventful - but still you're unhappy with how you see yourself.

You need to hear this good news: Someone very special loves you. His name is Jesus, and the proof that he loves you is conclusive: 2000 years ago Jesus came to this earth. His Father in Heaven sent Him, and He willingly came to carry out a specific task - to die - for you.

Jesus faced the most difficult task of all. One that God the Father considered necessary before he could adopt you. Yes, God wants you to be reborn into His family! And to bring that about, Father, Son and Holy Spirit agreed on a plan of salvation that would rid you of the sin which separates you from God.

God decided in advance to adopt us into his own family by bringing us to himself through Jesus Christ. This is what he wanted to do, and it gave him great pleasure (Ephesians 1:5). It is an awesome plan - but it requires sin to be dealt with. We all understand as children that when we do something wrong, we can expect punishment. If someone commits a crime, it is right that they are punished. So your sinful nature deserves punishment. Yet God loves you so much, and has such a desire to adopt you, that He chose to punish his only Son instead. Jesus suffered instead of you because He loved you. And God raised him from the dead to be your Saviour.

What now? You might reasonably ask, "Does God expect anything from me?" Just a simple act of faith; an acknowledgement that Jesus died for you; and a willingness to turn from sin and live for God. And by the single act of faith you can have all your sins forgiven and be adopted into God's family as His child. You may feel that your life is worthless, but you need to know that - "nobody is not loved" is actually true. God loves everybody. God loves YOU.
Anon.

24

I Could Blame God!

I was a pedestrian. Now I have no legs and I am not suitable for prosthesis. I was 'mown down' in the street by an out-of-control vehicle, estimated to be travelling at over forty miles an hour. As a result, my life and my family's life have been 'messed up.' The fact that it happens to others, too, is no consolation - it changes nothing for me.

So how do you think I feel about the person who did this to me? How would <u>you</u> feel? I'm glad I didn't die, and since recovering sufficiently to live a 'normal' life, I have found that many people are kind and helpful. I am surprised, however, how quickly some bring God into any discussions we have about what happened. One kind friend wrote, " How could God allow that to happen to a person like you?" They thought that because I am a Christian, God should have protected me.

In one paraphrased version of the Bible it says that "good luck and bad luck happen to everyone" (Ecclesiastes 9:11). So, although I'm a Christian, I know I must live my life like everyone else and accept what God allows. The difference for Christians in life's ups and downs is that God is with us. He enables us to handle our tragedies. God has given me a great sense of peace about that accident that changed my life. I don't blame God and I don't hate the car driver who dis this to me. Indeed, I have met with the man and assured him that I hold no hard feelings towards him.

At the root of my peace is the fact that I know Jesus of Nazareth as my Saviour. By believing in Him I received God's forgiveness for my own sins and entered into a new relationship with God. In all my anxieties God has been a Father to me and Jesus my Saviour a good friend. Let me share with you some verses from the Bible that, by assuring me of God's love and forgiveness, give me peace:

"Everyone who believes on him receives forgiveness of sins" (Acts 10:43).

"Jesus Christ of Nazareth, whom God raised from the dead ... Salvation is found in in no-one else, for there is no other name under heaven given to men by which we must be saved" (Acts 4:12).

"To all who received him [Jesus], to those who believed in his name, he gace the right to become children of God" (John 1:12).

Mary Kerr

25

Red Lines

Keep within the boundaries and all will be well! In one of the Middle East conflicts a red line was agreed: **no** chemical weapons to be used! Cross this red line and there **will** be consequences. However, chemical agents **were** used, and the threatened consequences **did not** happen! Political parties draw red lines to indicate polices on which they would never negotiate or compromise. Families and schools set red lines to indicate the boundaries of acceptable behavior. Crossing these red lines bring consequences like withdrawal of treats or expulsion from school.

God, our creator, has drawn red lines too! He drew one right at the beginning of mankind's history - under penalty of death - YOU MUST NOT EAT from a certain tree. The first man chose to disobey and "the rest is history"! All Mankind's problems can be traced back to that event. What God, in the Bible, calls "sin" came into the world. Through that red line being crossed and God's verdict is, **"All have sinned and fall short of the glory of God" (Romans 3:23).**

Can God ignore sin? No. What kind of judge would make light of law-breaking? God is the Judge of the entire world. But out of love for the people of the world, he did something to help us: He took the consequences of our sin on himself. By an act of mercy. God came into the world in the person of his Son Jesus who, having lived a perfectly obedient life, took the punishment that we deserved by dying on the cross. He paid a terrible price: suffering God's judgment for sin, though he himself was innocent and sinless, to prove that his death dealt effectively with sin and its consequence, God raised him from the dead!

This is how God brings us back to the right side of his red line - it is through repentance and faith. So, to reject God's offer of free salvation means we stay on the wrong side of that red line forever, while those who put their trust in Jesus have peace with God because of what Jesus Christ our Lord has done for us.

"Truly , I say to you, whoever hear my word and believes in him who sent me has eternal life. He does not come into judgment but has passed from death to life" (John 5:24).

Which side of the RED LINE are you on?
   Anon.

26

Christ is the Answer

There was once a shoemaker who, as he sat at work, came to think that when the pendulum of his clock swung to the left it said 'Forever' and when to the right it said 'Where.' He got up and stopped the clock! But although he had stopped the clock he discovered that the question was still in his mind, and he could not answer it. Many people of all ages have no answer to this question and like the shoemaker they try to silence it. But it cannot be silenced, for God has put 'Eternity' in our hearts. We are eternal for God made us this way. There is life after death. We cannot evade it. This is the appointment - **"man is destined to die once and after that to face judgement" (Hebrews 9:27).** The truth about man is that sin and unbelief in our lives have come between God and us. We no longer think of God or consider either His love for us or His righteous judgement of His Son. To dismiss the matter by hoping that there is no God, and no judgement day is no wiser than the shoemaker who stopped his clock to silence the question in his heart. God loves you and the proof of this is in the fact that He sent His Son to save you: **"For God so loved the world that He gave His one and only Son, that whosoever believes in Him shall not perish but have eternal life" (John 3:16)**. Jesus died for our sin and rose again from the dead to save from judgement all who call on Him. He is waiting for you. Say from your heart today, "Lord Jesus, I am a sinner, but you died for me. Thank you, Lord Jesus." (Anon.)

27

Motorway Madness

"A right smash up on the M1 today" said my colleague as he came on duty. I couldn't get his words out of my head as I travelled home and passed over the motorway to see the extent of the damage. As far as I could see there was the mangled wreckage cars, lorries and coaches. Police, ambulance and fire crews worked to sort the living from the dead. "Motorway Madness" the papers called it. Over 50 vehicles in a pile up in thick fog.

But wait, are you no better, even if you have never driven? The Bible tells us that the human race is plunging forwards in thick full fog, with a pile up at the end. Previous generations called it Hell; whatever you call it, the result is the same. Jesus Christ came into the world to save us from this pile-up: **"God did not send his Son into the world to condemn it, but to save it" (John 3:17).**

God sends no one to Hell - people are already on that route, because outside heaven there is nowhere else to go. There is no room in Heaven for a law breaker, and who can say that they have kept all of God's laws? We're all heading for the pile-up at the end of life unless we take action to avoid it.

If you turn from your sin and put your trust in Jesus Christ, you will know the joy and peace of fellowship with God in both this life and next. Listen to and turn away from the fog of folly and ignorance into the clear sunshine of God's love. Turn and put your trust in Jesus. Only he can save you from the carnage to come. And remember His love is free and unconditional: **"Those the Father has given me will come to me and I will never reject them"** (John **6:37).** No one is excluded from this offer. No one, however good can avoid the pileup without accepting it. **"The living God ... is the Saviour of all people"** **(Timothy 4:10).**

Anon.

28

Is Your Name Registered?

A lady was telling me recently of a beautiful church building in which all the names of her family are written on the walls. It must be nice for them to see this and know that their loved ones are not forgotten. No matter where your name may be written on this earth, if you want to live in heaven after you die there is a book being written there in which your name must be registered. The book is called 'The Lamb's Book of Life' (see Revelation 21:27). However, if your name is not written there, then tragically your destination is an awful place – 'The Lake of Fire' - where you will be forever (Revelation 20:15)! This is so serious that you must find out how you can have your name written in that book.

What is the Lamb's Book of Life? Jesus is called "the Lamb of God." He said: "I came that they might have life and have it abundantly" (John 10:10). By this he meant eternal life in Heaven. This is His book which records the names of all those who have accepted his gift of that life and thereby gain their citizenship in heaven.

How can I be sure my name is in the Lamb's Book of Life? John the Baptist said of Jesus, **"Behold the Lamb of God, who takes away the sin of the world!" (John 1:29)**. In those days lambs were sacrificed in the Jewish religion. An innocent animal died in place of guilty men and women so that they could be accepted before God. These, however, only symbolised Jesus who as the greatest sacrifice would do away with sin forever.

Jesus died in your place as the utterly sinless Lamb of God, **"... the Lord has laid on him the iniquity of us all" (Isaiah 53:6)**. So now, if you accept Jesus His Son as the sacrificial lamb who died for you, God will forgive your sins and you will have your name written in Heaven!

"Whoever believes in the Son has eternal life; whoever does not obey the Son shall not see life, but the wrath of God remains on him" (John 3:36).

Faith in Jesus is your passport to heaven. Take that step of believing in him today. Your name will be written in the Lamb's Book of Life, and you will be permanently registered as a citizen of heaven! Register now!
  Elsie Sands

29

Profit & Loss

"The value of your investment may go down as well as up and you may not recover all that you have invested."

We often see these words in advertisements offering great financial opportunities while at the same time giving a warning about the uncertainty of the future. None of us can see into the future and we don't know for certain what will happen to us - even during the next 24 hours. One person who wanted to make money and thought he saw what was ahead was Judas, a disciple of Jesus, who no doubt thought he had gained a secure financial future after he collected 30 pieces of silver to betray Jesus Christ. But he never recovered all that he had invested. He threw away the money and committed suicide. What he hadn't seen on that last day of his life was its tragic end.

"Do not store up for yourselves treasures on earth, where moth and rust destroy, and where thieves break in and steal. But store up for yourselves treasures in heaven ... For where your treasure is, there your heart will be also" (Matthew 6:19-21).

One thing is certain: God's word, the Bible, can be trusted. The Bible tells us that trust in the Lord Jesus and acceptance of his death on the cross for each one of us will bring us forgiveness for our sins so we will not face judgement.

"... He was pierced for our transgressions, he was crushed for our iniquities; the punishment that brought us peace was upon him, and by his wounds we are healed" (Isaiah 53:5).

"God demonstrates his own love for us in this: While we were still sinners, Christ died for us" (Romans 5:8).

God's love for you is shown through Jesus's death and resurrection. When you believe this your sins are forgiven, and eternal life is yours! God offers you great profit. To reject it is a terrible loss. **"What good will it be for a man if he gains the whole world, yet forfeits his soul?" (Matthew 16:26).**

Anon.

30

Too Late!

Why would any sensible person not make the time to think about the singularly most important thing in his life "Where will I spend eternity?"

- In boyhood he may be **too carefree**. He says: "There is plenty of time. No use bothering about these things now."
- In youth he is **too busy**. He has studies to occupy his time, and life to live for. He says: "I want to spend all the time that I can spare from sport and entertainment to make money." When I've settled down there will be time enough to think about religion."
- In manhood he is **too preoccupied**. Family responsibilities have to be faced. Business demands require urgent attention. He says: "I can't think of God yet; I need to deal with these serious matters first."
- In declining years **he feels too old**. His heart has become hardened to the ways of the world. Long-established habits are confirmed. He feels in a rut and can't get out of it.
- On his death bed **he is too ill**. He's in constant pain. He's totally preoccupied with his sufferings. His mind is going. He can't even concentrate anymore. There is no will power left.
- In death **he is too late**. Opportunity has gone. His spirit has left his body. According to the teaching of Christ there is now a fixed gulf between him and the eternal peace that might have been his. The offer of pardon and

salvation can never, ever be made to him.

As you read this, you must honestly face up to the question of your eternal future. That issue can be settled positively in your favour if you really want it. The way to settle it is through accepting the sacrifice of Christ upon the cross. He was there as the sin bearer, and the punishment for your sin was dealt to Him. that is what provides the way by which God - without treating sin lightly - can forgive and save you. if you put your trust in Christ, he will do this for you - right now! Is there any reason to delay?

Salvation is not a process to be gone through - it is a gift to be received. You can only receive it by faith in Christ. What prevents you from receiving it now?

"For God so loved the world that He gave His only begotten Son, that whoever believes in Him should not perish but have everlasting life" (John 3:16).

H.P. Barker

31

A Scientist Asks, "Is there a God?"

At school I was told that the Bible was 'unscientific' and that Jesus Christ never claimed to be the Son of God. My school days left me with the impression that Science would eventually solve all our problems. At university, I heard that 'sin' and 'evil' were outmoded ideas, and that environmental factors were the sole obstacle to man achieving an economic and social utopia. I am ashamed that I adopted these ideas without thinking and held them to my late 20s. Then, for the first time in my life, I began to think seriously about life and death, good and evil, the failure of human beings to live together in harmony, and the ultimate reason for human existence.

The first question I asked myself was "Is there a God?" It seemed impossible that the complex system of which we are such a small part could have come into being without a creator. Just as a great piece of music testifies to the skill of the composer, the world and the universe testified to the wisdom and power of God. Science is but a means to *describe* God's work. Two things occurred to me at this time.

The first was that there *was* evil in human beings -including me - and that this occurred naturally and wasn't learned. Secondly, is seemed likely to me that a human being *could* have some sort of personal contact with the creator of life. When I started to re-read the Bible - this time with an open mind -

it all fitted together like a jigsaw. Jesus *did* claim to be the Son of God. The Bible tells us that he died on a cross for our sins and rose again to a different dimension of divine life. He said, **"I am the Way, the Truth, and the Life" (John 14:6)** and, **"I am the Resurrection and the Life; anyone who believes in me will no longer be dead, but alive" (John 11:25).**

I discovered this vital life in Jesus when, at the age of almost thirty, I sought His forgiveness for all my sins. The change was radical, and complete. I find that the living Jesus Christ becomes more real to me day by day and I find in Him a source of peace and security which a mere scientific knowledge could never bring.

Professor Tony Holland, Salford University

32

No Satisfaction!

No Satisfaction is possibly the Rolling Stones' best-known single, with Sir Mick Jagger singing, "I can't get no satisfaction ... and I try ... and I try ... I can't get no satisfaction ..."

Are you like him: bored, fed up with nothing that gives real satisfaction, real peace? Are you always feeling that there's got to be something more? Well, there is ... His name is JESUS! Now don't dismiss this with a reflex reaction ... You may have been to church as a kid, or seen other people go to church, and seen them as no better than you. Going to church doesn't make you a Christian, anymore than sitting in the stands at a football match makes you a football player!

I don't want to tell you about a religion or a church, but about a man called Jesus, and about what He wants to give you - for free! As well as a life of satisfaction, there is also the promise of eternal life (see John 3:16). You see, Jesus was sent by God to prove how much He loves us. God sent Him to die, nailed to a cross on a hill outside Jerusalem about 2,000 years ago, yet He was an innocent man - it was a set-up.

The Bible tells us that we are all sinners (Romans 3:23) - that is, we're separated from God because we don't accept His love - and that what we do outside His love (sin) will result in our death (Romans 6:23). However, if we accept God's love for us, and His forgiveness for what we have done in our past, we can put our trust in His Son Jesus Christ as our Saviour. You don't need to have reached rock-bottom. A prisoner wrote recently:

> "*I tried to find peace through drink and drugs, but it wasn't there. I tried a life of crime, but ended up here. I even tried a tin of lighter fluid, but that scared me even more. I then looked at a book called the Bible ... That's where He lives, that's where I found Him. He set me free.*"

Jesus will set you free, and give you satisfaction and peace in this life – and the next.

Based on a tract by Graham Hair.

33

Christmas is for LIFE

The Dogs' Trust, (formerly the National Canine Defence League) has for many years carried a no-nonsense advertising slogan that says: 'A dog is for life, not just for Christmas.' The slogan was developed in response to the distressing rise in the number of abandoned dogs in the months soon after Christmas each year, when the novelty of owning a live animal wears off and the responsibility hits home, resulting in the "pets" being dumped. The purpose is to promote a responsible attitude to dog ownership, emphasising the commitment required to look after it for the rest of it's life.

We are horrified at the attitude of some people about Christmas pets, and yet our attitude to Christmas itself may be surprisingly similar! Don't we just love the Christmas festivities and fun, the presents and the puddings, the nativity plays and the carols? But when it's all over, we pack it all up and dump it unceremoniously, with all the trimmings, into the attic or the garage, for another year and, if we're honest, give a sigh of relief!

But actually, the significance of Christmas goes far beyond December 25th! The baby born in Bethlehem came to carry out God's life-changing plan to free us all from the deadly effect and consequences of our sin (John 3:16). Even though it meant that, to remove our death sentence and bring us eternal life He would have to give His *own* life, Jesus made that selfless commitment to achieve that goal (1 Peter 2:24). If we might put it another way - **Christmas is for life!**

One of the traditions of Christmas that children particularly enjoy is giving and receiving gifts. Another is the nativity play where we hear the angel announcing God's gift to the world, **"Today ... a Saviour has been born to you" (Luke 2:11).** The question is - what are you going to do with this gift?

To accept Jesus, that is to receive him inwardly through belief or faith, makes you part of God's family - a child of God (John 1:12). You could ignore it like a discarded puppy or your boxed-up decorations - but *this* Christmas, why not accept God's gift of eternal life through Jesus Christ (Romans 6:23)?

Anon.

34

Is It 'Nothing' To You?

A 30-foot-high sculpture by artist David Mach adorns the entrance to Morrison's supermarket in the Scottish town of Kirkcaldy in Fife. It is crafted from pieces of driftwood which he collected on the beach. Thousands of steel tacks have been hammered into it to catch the light. According to sculptor Mach, the piece is abstract and represents 'nothing in particular' - except perhaps the hardy spirit of the people of Fife. He said, "it's the ugliest thing I have ever done ... but I like it a lot." Inevitably, local opinions are divided! Some like it, some don't, and others couldn't care less. Their opinions about it are unlikely to be life changing. The cross of Christ is the ugliest thing ever done by man. He was crucified because he revealed the ugly truth about a rebellious nature. Yet at the cross, God's love is seen in all its beauty. In spite of man's cruelty, Jesus offered himself to God as a sin atoning sacrifice for a guilty world. **"For God so loved the world, that he gave his only Son, that whoever believes in him should not perish but have eternal life" (John 3:16). "Is it nothing to you, all you who pass by?" (Lamentations 1:12).**

Our response to Christ's death on the cross will affect us forever. Nails driven into a tree; Light of the world, You died there for me.

Jo Johnson

35

What's Wrong With This Country?

What's wrong? Consider these four points:

1. The alarming increase of violence and defiance of authority. We are constantly faced with joy riding, car theft, hooliganism, armed robbery, brutal murders, cold-blooded bombings and terrorism.
2. The sickening speed of sexual offences. Fed by pornographic literature and films; exploited by advertisers and pop culture, society has become sex-mad, its attitude corrupted, and its healthy inhibitions undermined.
3. Insane expenditure on gambling or pleasure. At a time when the nation is fighting for its life, millions of pounds are sunk into betting and self-gratification. The major concern of many is how to get 'kicks' out of life.
4. The religious indifference that prevails. The Bible is an unknown book and religion is largely despised. On the other hand, false religions, false cults, black magic and Devil worship proliferate.

What can I do? Well, quite a lot in fact. A nation is made-up of individuals, so if you want things to become better, begin with yourself. "I've tried" you confess. And failed. But Jesus Christ can succeed where you have failed. He can change your life so here's what to do: First: you must acknowledge your need of God. One man put it like this: **"God be merciful to me, a sinner"**

(Luke 18:13). Then believe that he can meet your need. The Bible says, **"God so loved the world, that He gave his only begotten Son, that whosoever believes upon Him should not perish, but have everlasting life"** (John 3:16). Thirdly, accept Jesus Christ as your own Saviour and Lord; **"But as many as received Him to them he gave the power to become the sons of God, even to them that believe on His name"** (John 1:12).

A. Linford

36

How Many Dots?

Have you heard of a film "The Third Man?" It's about Holly Martin's search through Vienna in the aftermath of the Second World War for his friend, Harry Lime. Having faked his own death, Lime now has a racket stealing penicillin and selling it on the black market. Appalled at the suffering of those who will die without treatment as a result, Martin wants nothing to do with it. In an unforgettable scene, Harry Lime takes him up on a Ferris wheel and points to the scurrying crowds in the fairground below: "Look down there. Tell me, would you really feel any pity if one of those dots stop moving forever? If I offered you £20,000 for every dot that stopped, would you really, old man, tell me to keep my money? Or would you calculate how many dots you could afford to spare?"

It seems, if you are far enough away, people lose their individuality. You can stop caring. What does God see when he looks down from Heaven? Seven billion dots swarming about? Does he even notice when one of them stops moving? When one of them is hurting? Jesus said: **"Are not two sparrows sold for a penny? Not yet not one of them will fall to the ground apart from the will of your Father. And even the very hairs of your head are all numbered. So don't be afraid; You are worth more than many sparrows"** (Matthew 10:29-31).

You are of value to God! He values you so much that He was prepared to give up His own Son to rescue you. One of the Bible writers realised it and wrote: **"The life I live in the body, I live by faith in the Son of God who loved me and gave himself up for me" (Galatians 2:20).** When the Lord Jesus died on the cross, He took the punishment for your sins so that you wouldn't have to take it yourself: He had you - personally - in mind! So you are certainly not a forgettable dot! If you trust in your heart - even as you are reading this - that He really did die for you, then you will be saved from your sins and begin a new life with him.

Karl Smith

37

How to Be Rich

On June 1764, Letizia Romalino married a lawyer named Carlo. They eventually had 13 children, 5 of whom died in infancy. Of the surviving children, one became a Grand Duchess; one a Princess; one a Queen; three became Kings and one became an Emperor. The Emperor was Napoleon Bonaparte, and it was on this brother's coat tails that Letizia's other children rose to high position and immense wealth. Letizia never forgot the family's humble origins, and counselled her children about their attitude to fame and fortune: "... just as long as it lasts," she would say. She knew that life was full of uncertainties and that wealth was no guarantee of happiness. After his defeat at Waterloo, Napoleon's titles and wealth were lost.

Jesus once told a story about a rich farmer, who, realising how wealthy he was, planned to retire to enjoy his money, but died before he could do so. (Luke 12:15-21) The point of the story was not only that life is uncertain, but that the farmer had become greedy. In his drive to obtain wealth, he disregarded God and what lay beyond this life. As Jesus said, he was **"not rich towards God" (Luke 12:21).**

How can you be rich towards God? The key is Jesus Christ. Here is what the Bible says about Him: **"... though he was rich, yet for your sakes he became poor, so that you through his poverty might become rich" (2 Corinthians**

8:9). Before He came to this world Jesus was rich. As God's Son He was always in God's presence, sharing the glory of heaven. In coming to earth He chose to live as a poor man. It was in this lowly state that He went to the cross to bear your sin and mine: ***"And being found in appearance as a man, he humbled himself and became obedient to death – even death on a cross!"*** **(Philippians 2:3).**

Jesus' sacrifice makes possible the exchange mentioned earlier: **"that you through his poverty might become rich,"** rich in the way Jesus was before He came to this world. TO LIVE IN THE LIGHT OF GOD'S PRESENCE FOREVER, WHAT MORE COULD WE WISH FOR? THAT IS BEING RICH; RICH TOWARD GOD.

Anon.

38

The Danger Tree

The Danger Tree is located in the First World War Newfoundland Memorial Park at Beaumont, Hamel, France. The Danger Tree is a replica of an original tree and marks the place where the Royal Newfoundland Regiment sustained dreadful losses on the opening day of the Battle of the Somme. After the first day of the battle, allied soldiers knew that the tree indicated the place in no-man's-land where they were within range of enemy machine gunfire; to pass beyond it meant danger. Yet that same tree, if passed in the opposite direction after a failed attack would mark the point beyond which enemy fire could not reach. The same tree meant something different depending on the direction of approach.

The Bible, in certain places, describes the cross of Jesus as a tree. It, too, is a tree that means something different depending on how you approach it. For many it is a warning, a danger tree. For others it is a place of protection and healing, a safety tree. Are you someone who views the death of Jesus from a sceptical point of view? Then to you the cross sounds a warning: **"Christ redeemed us … by becoming a curse for us, for it is written: 'Cursed is everyone who is hung on a tree'" (Galatians 3:13).**

In what sense was Jesus cursed? He was cursed because on the cross he was bearing the punishment due from God for all the sins of humankind. It was there that God's righteous anger and unerring justice were satisfied in regard to sin. To the unbeliever the Cross sounds a warning that there is an ultimate cost to human sin, and that God will call everyone to account because of it. To the sceptic the Cross of Jesus is a danger tree.

To the person who believes that in Jesus Christ God has provided the basis of forgiveness of sin, the Cross is a safety tree. **"He himself bore our sins in his body on the tree ... by his wounds you have been healed" (1 Peter 2:24).** It is the place where believers find that their sin has already been paid for, and the rift between themselves and God has been healed. To them the Cross of Jesus is a symbol of eternal safety. It is proof that someone already has already died for their sins. What is your approach to the Cross of Christ? For you is it a 'danger tree' or a 'safety tree'?

Anon.

39

Beyond Hope

On the US highway in Arizona there is a tiny village called Hope - it boasts only a grocery store and a 2-pump gas station. You could easily drive past without noticing it! Someone erected a sign on the side of the road that reads "Beyond Hope," with the intention of raising a smile on the motorist's face, and it has! It raises not only smiles, but serious thoughts too, for some have said: "That's me! I'm beyond hope ..." It's surprising how many people feel like that.

Life turns sour sometimes, huge disappointments in family or business, broken health, maybe through mental illness. There seems no end to the long dark tunnel. Whatever the cause, of our own making or not, it is tough and easy to lose hope. The Bible confirms that. In fact it uses the expression **"without hope and without God" (Ephesians 2:12)** - the two go together. If we are without God we are without hope, but we do not need to be without God. He is our maker, and He cares for us: **"He himself gives all men life and breath and everything else" (Acts 17:25).**

Sin has raised a terrible barrier between us, and God and we are all sinners. We have all broken God's laws. Because we break them God seems far away and life seems hopeless though it need not be like this, you are not beyond hope. Honestly you are not! The Bible says **"the God of hope fill you with**

**all joy and peace as you trust in him, so that you may overflow with hope"
(Romans 15:13).** Joy and peace - surely that is what you want? God wants to
give them to you and His gifts are lasting and real. He gives peace that does
not come and go with life's ups and downs, and joy deep in the heart. Life
does not need to be hopeless.

The Bible promises that there is a hope held out in the gospel **(Colossians
1:23).** The gospel is God's good news and concerns his Son, Jesus Christ. He
came to be our Saviour and He died on a cross to bear the punishment for
our sins. God asks us to believe in Him and to receive His gift of eternal life,
**"The wages of sin is death, but the gift of God is eternal life in Christ Jesus
our Lord" (Romans 6:23**). The little village of Hope lies at the crossroads of
highways 60 and 72. Maybe God is bringing you to the crossroads of life. If
you hear His word, acknowledge that you are a sinner and put your trust in
Jesus Christ as your Saviour, you will find your heart will overflow with hope.
It will, for that is His promise and God always keeps his promises.
  Anon.

40

Seek Assistance

A friend of mine was travelling on the London Underground the other day with a ticket that had been printed incorrectly when he had bought it. He could get *into* the underground okay, but when he tried to leave the station at his destination, the barrier wouldn't let him through! The sign came up "Invalid Ticket, Seek Assistance." Which he did – and the station staff let him through. But the same thing happened the next day and the day after that … so he checked with the station where he had got his ticket, to be told that the printing machine had an intermittent fault and failed to print the instructions to allow the ticket holder *out* through the barrier.

This made me think about life's journey. How often do we go through our life without the right ticket to exit at the end of it – and even when we are told to "Seek Assistance" we don't do it, or we asked the wrong person. The Christian believes that there are three reliable sources of assistance we can seek. Firstly, the Bible (still the world's bestselling book), where Jesus says, **"I am the way and the truth and the life. No one comes to the Father except through me" (John 14:6).** The words in this book are the best written guide to our lives. Secondly, there are Christians that have travelled this way before us and may well have similar experiences that can help us through. Thirdly, the big news is that there is a personal assistant available for each one of us. The Bible calls him the Holy Spirit. When we pray to God, it's the Holy Spirit who communicates back to us, guiding our conscience, giving us insight into what we should do or say in any situation.

These are all available to everyone who accepts Jesus as their Saviour. So why not acknowledge that you *need His Assistance* to please God, and you will find that Jesus will help you find the right path through life, and you can also be confident of the only safe exit to eternity!

Mark Walford

41

Time Is Running Out

Our world is changing - what does the future hold in store? Climate change is not just an environmental issue, it's also a threat to people living in poverty. Global warming is already happening, and scientists are certain human activity is the cause. While rich nations contribute most to climate change, poor communities struggle to adapt to its devastating effects. Many people die every year from the health impacts of climate change. By the end of the century, rising sea levels and crop failures could result in millions of refugees. God cares about the damage we're doing to the planet and our lack of care for the poor who suffer the effects. The Bible confirms that changes are coming upon this world, some clearly as a result of humankind's increasing carelessness and evil, and some the judgments of God on our world not listening to His word: **"There will be earthquakes in various places, and famines" (Mark 13:8).** The world is changing rapidly, and time is running out! The good news is that God has provided a way of deliverance for us all that we may escape. This deliverance is through the Son of God, the Lord Jesus Christ, **"who gave himself for our sins to rescue us from the present evil age" (Galatians 1:4).** Take the opportunity to change your own destiny by accepting the deliverance available to you through the Lord Jesus Christ. **"For God so loved the world that he gave his one and only Son, that whoever believes in him shall not perish but have eternal life" (John 3:16).** Anon.

42

Xmas or Christmas?

Where did the 'X' come from? Did it just make a long word shorter? The X is useful. It's quick and easy to write "Merry Xmas" so it saves time. It's quick and easy on a text message on your mobile phone. But that's not how it began. There's another reason. 'X' comes from the first letter of the Greek word for 'Christ.'

The first letter looks like an X. The 'X' was first used by the Greeks who knew what it stood for: but did you? This was just a shorthand when many educated people understood Greek and knew what it stood for; but did you? Some children were asked, "What's Christmas all about?" and they eagerly replied, "Presents and holidays and chocolates." They had to be asked if there was anything else. Then they remembered Jesus.

A lot of adults aren't much different. 'X' is the unknown; yet the coming of Christ into the world was the most important event in the world's history. A remembrance of it can be gently appealing, as we think of Jesus as a little baby, but we miss the point if we don't think of its purpose. When He was born, the angel said about His mother, **"she will give birth to a son, and you are to give him the name Jesus, because He will save His people from their sins" (Matthew 1:21).** Christ was born in order to give Himself to die, instead of us who deserved to die, because we had sinned against God.

- "God demonstrated his own love for us in that whilst we were still sinners, Christ died for us" (Romans 5:8).
- "Christ died for our sins according to the scriptures" (1 Corinthians 15:3).
- "For the wages of sin is death, but the gift of God is eternal life in Christ Jesus our Lord" (1 John 5:12).
- "He who has the Son has life; he who does not have the Son of God does not have life" (Matthew 1:21).

Peter Hickling

43

What Is Success?

Why did Jay Gould, once one of America's richest men, exclaim as he lay dying: "I'm the most miserable man in the world!"? Because money has no power to satisfy man's deepest needs. He who trades his soul's biggest interests for wealth makes a poor bargain. Money cannot buy salvation or assure the future.

History tells us that Alexandra the Great, when the then whole world was under his rule, wept at the misfortune that his exploits must cease, as there were no more worlds to conquer. Why? Because success and gratified ambition can never give you lasting satisfaction. Even Alexander, the hero of so many battles was at last to fall before the grim power of death. Only Christ can fill the heart with lasting joy.

Why did one of the England's finest poets, Lord Byron cry out on his death bed: "My days are in yellow leaf, the fruit of life, the flower is gone: the worm, the canker, and the grief are mine alone" Because genius and popular acclaim are powerless to give us what we really need. A personal knowledge of the love of Christ is worth more than anything else.

Why did a well-known religious professor cry out with his dying breath: "I am going to hell!"? Because he realised, too late, that religion without Jesus

Christ is empty and worse than worthless. In the face of death and eternity, religion is revealed as a delusion and as a hollow sham if it does not have a personal experience of Jesus Christ as Saviour at its centre.

Why did a prison warden, frightened by a severe earthquake ask one of his prisoners, he knew to be a Christian: **"What must I do to be saved?" (Acts 16:30).** Because he saw that nothing matters more when the chips are down, to be saved is the most vital thing that can happen to anyone. Jesus, the Saviour said of his teaching: **"These things I say, so that you can be saved" (John 5:34).**

As you read this, why don't you find this Jesus Christ, be saved, find satisfaction in life, and assurance of eternity with him in heaven? **"If you confess with your mouth the Lord Jesus, and believe in your heart that God raised him from the dead, you shall be saved" (Romans 10:9).**

Based on a tract by H.P. Barker

44

The Message in the Snow

After 49 days of pain, starvation and loneliness on a snow-covered mountain in British Columbia a man and a woman are alive to tell their story, which is probably unequalled in the annals of Canada's far north ; and the survival of the couple—both American citizens—is considered by those who have a knowledge of Canada's vast hinterland to be nothing short of a miracle. It was a giant-sized S.O.S. which took three days to scrape out in the snow that led to their rescue. This mute appeal, coupled with a large arrow laboriously dug out of the snow to indicate their position, was seen from the air by an alert pilot, who landed close by and effected a thrilling rescue.

S.O.S. - how often this message has been sent by those in distress! On many occasions the message has not been heard, or seen, or it was unheeded, and tragedy has resulted. This has been especially frequent at sea. The Federal Department of Transport urge all who journey into the far north to go prepared. Travelers require sufficient warm clothing, sleeping bags, food, and other essentials such as flares for distress signals. Yet many pay no heed and make this journey unprepared! Such was the case with this man and woman, and for 42 of the 49 days they were sustained only by melted snow, an ordeal preparation could have saved.

Many are equally unprepared for life's journey, and the eternity that lies beyond. Dear reader, please consider this timely warning, consider your latter end. "Now for a leap into the dark" were words said to have been uttered by Ingersoll, the infidel, shortly before he departed this life. He who had lectured across the Continent on his unbelief in God's existence realized that he was unprepared for this inevitable end to life's journey.

So many people are quite complacent concerning eternal issues. They go through life oblivious of the loving Saviour who gave His blood to save them. They appear confident that they can live without Him, but the tragedy is they die without Christ, and so they end the journey and pass into eternity—lost forever.

It is true the entreaties of many who have signaled an S.O.S. have been in vain, but should you realize your peril of being unprepared to pass into the vast eternity, be assured your cry for salvation will certainly be heard by the Lord. He is faithful to His promise, and His promise is:

> **"If thou shalt confess with thy mouth the Lord Jesus, and shalt believe in thine heart that God hath raised Him from the dead, thou shalt be saved." Further He says, "Whosoever shall call upon the name of the Lord shall be saved" (Romans 10:9,13 KJV).**

Fred Lundwill

<h1 style="text-align:center">45</h1>

Great Discovery

What was the greatest discovery in the field of medicine over the last 200 years or so? Could it be anaesthetics? We all owe a debt to Dr James Simpson who originated the use of ether as an anaesthetic in midwifery in 1847. The same year he discovered something he thought better in chloroform. Perhaps it was antiseptics? It was Lord Joseph Lister who in 1860 revolutionised modern surgery by the introduction of the modern antiseptic's system. On the other hand, maybe it's antibiotics – without doubt many people will consider this the greatest discovery in medicine. In 1928 Sir Alexander Fleming discovered by accident the first penicillin, though it was 1942 before it was produced on a large scale.

These were great discoveries, instrumental in saving countless numbers of lives, but there was a greater discovery. It was only in the middle of the eighteenth century that the serious nature of dirt was realised; that it was dirt that carried and spread disease; that dirt was the unseen agent hindering and preventing healing. Today both medicine and surgery insist on cleanliness. Now what dirt is to the body (an enemy and potential killer), so sin is to the soul, to the personality, to our whole being.

Dirt is universal and no respecter of persons, and so is sin: **"... for all have sinned and come short of the glory of God" (Romans 3:23).** If dirt can maim so can sin: **"one who sins against me injures himself" (Proverbs 8:36 NASB).** Dirt, if it is ignored or neglected, may even prove fatal – the same is certainly true with sin. The solution to the problem of dirt lies in cleanliness, in hygiene, and in the use of antiseptics and antibiotics. But has the solution been found to the problem of sin? The answer is in emphatically yes, and it is a divine solution, not one concocted by man. The Bible tells us that **"Jesus Christ came into the world to save sinners" (1 Timothy 1:15).** He did this when he died on the cross, not only bearing our sins in his body, but also bearing our punishment.

I began by asking a question concerning discovery; let me ask you another one. Have you discovered that it is possible for you to be pardoned and forgiven by a holy God? Have you discovered the truth that **"the blood of Jesus Christ, his Son, cleanses us from all sin" (1 John 1:7)**? The actual discovery and experience of these things lie in our obedience to the Bible which declares: **"... let the wicked forsake his way, and the unrighteous man his thoughts, and let him return unto the Lord, and He will have mercy upon him, and to our God, for He will abundantly pardon" (Isaiah 55:7).**

Anon.

46

Wanted

My landlord has thrown me out ... he doesn't want me. I've been made redundant ... my boss doesn't want me. My husband has left me ... he doesn't want me. My skin's the wrong colour ... nobody wants me. My children never visit me ... nobody wants me. I'm living on my own ... nobody wants me. I am old ... nobody wants me. Have you ever felt like this? Do you ever feel that nobody really wants you? Do not despair! There is someone who wants to know you more than you would ever think possible. Jesus Christ, the Son of God, lived on this earth to show his love for you. But during His life 2000 years ago very few people wanted to know Him: **"He was despised and rejected by men, a man of sorrows, and familiar with suffering" (Isaiah 53:3).** Yet He wanted you so much that He let His enemies put Him to death. When He suffered and died on the cross, He took on himself your guilt and sin. **"God made him who had no sin to be sin for us" (2 Corinthians 5:21).** By taking our guilt on Himself, He took away the barrier that separates you from God. When you thank God for Jesus who died for your sins, God is pleased to forgive you. God wants to hear you speak to Him. **"Anyone who comes to him must believe that he exists and that he rewards those who earnestly seek him" (Hebrews 11:6).** Jesus said, **"Come to me, all you who are weary and burdened, and I will give you rest" (Matthew 11:28).** He wants to come into your life and be your friend - won't you welcome Him?

Anon.

47

The Eyewitness

"Once upon a time there was an old king who had three sons …" so begins our typical tale from bygone days! Storytelling is an ancient tradition, enjoyed the world over! You will have your own favourite story from yesteryear. Mine is the Arthurian legends, with King Arthur, Camelot, the Round Table and Excalibur; I love the deeds of valour in an atmosphere of forests and mists. Yet, although they are exciting, these tales like all the others are merely legends.

The only exception is a story concerning the Life and Times of Jesus Christ, the Son of God. His life has been recorded independently in the Bible by the gospel writers, Matthew, Mark, Luke, and John. The first three of these narrators described vividly how that one-day Jesus went up a mountain where His face became a radiant and glorious light, as bright as the sun. A voice then came from Heaven, saying **"This is my Son, whom I love. Listen to Him" (Mark 9:7).**

One of the eyewitnesses to this incident was Simon Peter, a follower of Jesus. Later in life he wrote about this incident: **"We did not follow cleverly invented stories when we told you about the power and coming of our Lord Jesus Christ, but we were eyewitnesses of His Majesty" (2 Peter 1:16).** Peter's witness still stands what he saw was no deception, nor is it a myth today.

Peter also wrote concerning the Lord Jesus Christ: **"He himself bore our sins in his body on the tree, so that we might die to sins and live for righteousness; by his wounds you have been healed"** (1 Peter 2:24). Peter not only witnessed the glory of the Lord Jesus Christ on a mountain but also his sufferings when he was executed on a wooden cross. Then after Jesus' bodily resurrection and before His return to heaven where He is today, Peter also saw him again.

All of these awe-inspiring events were God's plan to declare His Son as who He was and is, "Jesus the Son of God," the Saviour of sinful people. Your eternal future is now at stake, and it depends on how you respond to the death of Christ. He paid the penalty for your sins so that you might be set free from the slavery of sin and have the free gift of eternal life. If you believe that Jesus died for you and if you ask God to forgive your sins, you will be saved for eternity. But if you do not believe, God will reject you. God wants you to be saved so much that He gave His own Son for you. Accept the testimony of Peter, the eyewitness: **"Christ died for sins once for all, the righteous for the unrighteous, to bring you to God"** (1 Peter 3:18).

Anon.

48

Dam Buster

The Lancaster heavy bombers of Royal Air Force 617 squadron breached the giant German dams in May 1943. The special cylindrical bouncing bombs - though huge by the standards of the day - were only able to weaken the colossal structures. What toppled the dams was the pent-up force of the water behind them. The raid was timed to coincide with a maximum volume of water contained in the dams. The effort cost many lives, both of aircraft and civilians, with a significant psychological impact on both sides. Sometimes in our lives a dam bursts. Pent-up emotions burst, out of control, when something triggers the collapse of restraint. As with Germany in 1943 such outpouring is destructive, and the landscape is changed forever. Personal loss and destroyed relationships are the resulting scars. The biggest destructive forces in our lives today are doubt and guilt. We do not know what to believe. We feel we are flawed structures under great pressure. When highly stressed we feel ready to crack up. One pent-up destructive flood we do not need to fear is judgement for our failures. Failing to do what is right is sin and God dealt with that once and forever when Jesus died for you on the cross of Calvary. **"All your waves and breakers have swept over me" (Psalm 42:7)** is how one translation of the Bible describes it. Do not crack up under the stresses and strains of life's pressures. Accept today what Jesus did for you and you can have the certainty of relief from the unbearable burden of sin. **"He himself bore our sins in his body on the tree" (1 Peter 2:24).** (Anon.)

49

Hidden Slavery

Most people in first world countries think that slavery was ended in the 19th century. Today international law declares slavery illegal, yet it still survives hidden under different guises: bonded labour and people trafficking. The UN estimates that upwards of 20 million people are held in some form of slavery; some estimate it as high as 200 million. Although it is illegal, slavery is a reality for millions.

Jesus Christ warned of a slavery that affects the whole human race; a slavery that has a bearing on the eternal well-being of the soul; a slavery that is hidden deep in the human heart. Jesus once said to a group of listeners: **"If you hold to my teaching ... then you will know the truth, and the truth will set you free" (John 8:31,32).** This remark raised a storm of protest among his audience, who insisted that they were free men. Jesus replied: **"I tell you the truth, everyone who sins is a slave to sin" (John 8:34).** Jesus was pointing out that no one is really free, for there is within everyone a capacity to do wrong, an urge so strong that it can be said to enslave us. No matter how strong-willed he or she may be, no one is immune from sinful thoughts or deeds. This fact has created a huge gulf between the Holy and Righteous God of heaven and sinful men and women.

To his listeners, Jesus gave the illustration of a rich household of those days.

In such a household domestic slaves had no real authority or freedom, but the Son and heir of the household had authority to decide major issues including setting slaves free. Jesus concluded with the words: **"So if the Son sets you free, you will be free indeed" (John 8:34).** He was in effect saying that he, Jesus, as Son of God had the authority to set people free from the slavery of sin. But what about our sins: surely a just and holy God cannot simply sweep mankind's failings under the carpet?

As well as freedom, God through his Son provided the remedy for sin. He didn't just ignore it. It had to be punished, but the Lord Jesus willingly allowed himself to be punished for all the sins you have done and that have held you in slavery throughout your life. The Bible says about Jesus: **"... he has appeared once for all ... to do away with sin by the sacrifice of himself" (Hebrews 9:26).** This means that the following invitation is extended to all humankind: **"... that everyone who believes in him receives the forgiveness of sins through his name" (Acts 10:43).** Will you accept by faith the invitation to freedom and forgiveness that Jesus has made possible through his death?

Anon.

50

Little Donkey

The Christmas song "Little Donkey" was made popular in the 1960s by Nina and Frederick, a husband and wife singing duo from Denmark. The lyrics of the song create a charming picture of a little donkey carrying Mary to Bethlehem where Christ was born. The Bible does not actually say that Mary rode a donkey to Bethlehem. It is a reasonable assumption that she did, for in biblical times the donkey was a common beast of burden, and a means of transport that even the poor could afford.

It may only be a supposition that Jesus was carried on a donkey, while in the womb of his mother, to Bethlehem the place of his birth. However the Bible specifically states that Jesus rode on a donkey on his last visit to Jerusalem, the place of his death (see Luke 19:28-36). The donkey that Jesus rode was a young colt that had never carried anything before. Possibly the donkey was subsequently employed on the great trade routes of the Middle East. Even if he carried treasures of gold and jewels, that little beast of burden would never carry a more precious load than when he carried Jesus into Jerusalem.

For when the donkey bore Jesus, not only was he carrying the King of Kings, but he was carrying the greatest burden bearer who had ever lived. This is what the Bible says about Jesus: **"Surely he took up our infirmities and carried our sorrows for he bore the sins of many" (Isaiah 53:4,12). "He**

himself bore our sins in his body on the tree" (1 Peter 2:24). We cannot imagine the magnitude of the Lord Christ carried at Calvary when he bore the weight of human sin. We can however experience the relief of having the burden of our sin and guilt taken away. Here is a personal invitation from Jesus to each one of us: **"Come to me, all you who are weary and burdened, and I will give you rest" (Matthew 11:28).**

Anon.

51

Why Do They Do It?

What motivates an Olympic athlete? Why do they endure years of training: special diets, physical preparation, mental conditioning and so much more? Today, due to close-up TV coverage, we see the expression on the face of the winner at the very moment of victory. They are elated! *Jubilant!* That moment - and all that follows - is why they do it!

No Olympic competitor goes into the games thinking it will cost them their life. If they did, their motivation to compete would have to be very different and of a much greater kind. The Bible says of Jesus Christ **"... who for the joy set before him endured the cross, scorning its shame ..." (Hebrews 12:2).** Death by crucifixion was cruel and painful. Why did he do it? His motivation _was_ very different to the Olympian. It was His incredible love for humankind whom he wanted to rescue. The Bible makes it clear that no one has any merit in God's eyes, **"For all have sinned and fall short of the glory of God" (Romans 3:23)** and **"... gratifying the cravings of our sinful nature and following its desires and thoughts ... we were by nature objects of wrath" (Ephesians 2:3).**

Our flawed nature makes us the objects of God's retribution. We need help! What Jesus did on the cross that day was to bear, in our place, the full force of God's just anger! This makes it possible for God to forgive us for our sins, because someone else (Jesus) has taken all the punishment already. If we have faith to accept that Jesus suffered on our behalf, we have complete forgiveness and eternal life, as this quote from the Bible says: **"Whoever believes in the Son has eternal life, but whoever rejects the Son will not see life, for God's wrath remains on him" (John 3:36).**

Anon.

52

They Think It's All Over!

They thought it was all over, and just like the crowd at a famous football match around 1966 years later, they started celebrating early... the troublesome preacher and teacher was gone. They had won, their plans had succeeded. The false charges and gentle persuasion of a local politician to sign the death warrant had all worked beyond their expectations. The threat to their positions in society, their power and authority was gone. But they were wrong ... The second half was only just starting ... The second half saw his resurrection, witnessed by many at the time, and believed since by literally billions of people across the world through the centuries that followed.

The man murdered was Jesus Christ, the one who said then, and says to you now: **"Greater love has no man than to give his life for his friends, and you are my friends" (John 15:13)**. Why did He have to die? The answer is so that we do not have to face the punishment due to us. What punishment? Isn't being a good person enough? No. The Bible says that all have fallen short of God's standards (see Romans 3:23). If God is perfect (and if he wasn't, he wouldn't be God) then anything less than perfection is failure. Failure has a price, in this case eternal separation from God, His love and all that is good in life. That's what we have called "the wages of sin" and the separation "hell."

Jesus' death, in some way we cannot understand, means that he has paid that price for us, been our substitute, taken our place, so we can be seen by God as perfect, despite our imperfections. The cross speaks of His sacrifice, the empty tomb of His power and continuing influence in the world today. The empty tomb has the final word ... they think it's all over ... it is now!

Anon.

53

How Do You Find Life?

Is it getting better? Or has it turned sour? Is it a thrilling adventure? Or a drab existence? Just the dull grind of routine, eating, drinking and sleeping with just the occasional little bit of fun thrown in from time to time? Do you know that you can be on top of the world, without needing other things? Read these words: **"Whoever is born of God overcomes the world; and this is the victory that overcomes the world, even our faith. Who is he that overcomes the world, but he that believes that Jesus is the Son of God?" (1 John 5:4).** Overcoming the world, getting on top of it, is a problem we all face and this is the only solution. When someone is "born of God" they begin to share the life of God, winning over failure and circumstances. Jesus Christ, God's Son, defeated sin and death when he died and came back to life again. **"Everyone who receives him, gets the power to become a Son of God by birth from above" (John 1:12,13).** You can be on top of the world. Receive Jesus Christ by faith, then the very life of God will become yours. It's not just a new start in life, but something even better, a new life to start with. That's why the Bible calls it often "new birth." Get on top of the world. Believe on the son of God. He promises: **"He who comes to me I will not cast out" (John 6:37)** Then come! Acknowledge before God that you are not the person you ought to be. Turn from your sin to the Lord Jesus Christ and ask him to takeover and guide your life from now on.

H.A. Gilpin

54

Blood Freely Given

For years I have been a Blood Donor. It was a real achievement to be awarded by *'Gold'* badge! The Doctor who presented it said, "When you started donating, it may have been your wish to save some lives. Well you've done that and more. Your blood type is used in the Premature Baby Packs. Already you have saved fifty babies' lives." I immediately thought, "God didn't give me babies of my own but He has allowed me to save fifty babies!" I cried all the way home and was forced to wear my sunglasses even though the rain was pouring down! I got some odd looks at the bus stop!

Recently I was invited to donate bone marrow. The patient who needed it had leukaemia. In the end, my samples were inadequate and another donor was a better match so I was reinstated as a platelet donor and discovered I had enough platelets for a treble dose. The doctor joked that as they'd had nothing from me for several months, it was the least I could do!

The main point in all this is that *nothing at all is required from the patient,* other than to accept the donated blood, believing it will give them a new lease of life. Did you know that the most precious blood of all – spotless and sinless – was freely given for you by the Lord Jesus Christ when He died on the cross?

"...you were ransomed not with perishable things such as silver or gold,

but with the precious blood of Christ, like that of a lamb without blemish or spot."[1]

The price for our sins was paid in blood – Christ's blood. All He asks of you is to accept that He took the blame for all your sins and by being punished in your place, blotted them out forever. If you invite Jesus into your life, you will confidently be able to say: **"In him we have redemption through his blood, the forgiveness of our trespasses, according to the riches of his grace."[2]**

Anon.

References are from: (1) 1 Peter 1:18-19; (2) Ephesians 1:7

55

What Then? What Now?

Today with cheaper flights, special offers, Air Miles, saving by Internet booking and cutthroat competition, it's no small wonder that millions of people fly across the world. If you've been an air traveller you will have shared with others the exhilaration of all that is involved in the approach to your destination: fastening your seat belt, feeling your ears popping, perhaps wondering if relatives or friends will be at the airport to meet you and observing the descent through the clouds. Suddenly there comes into sight the panoramic view of your destination, and many first-time travellers are surprised to see row upon row of houses, looking like lines of little boxes.

We all use boxes in our day-to-day lives, whether at school, college, work or home, the most sophisticated of these being computers and televisions. Our descent by plane causes us to realise that our houses are really only boxes as well. So whether we think of the functional cardboard box, the computer, the television or our house, they are effectively all boxes of different shapes and sizes. These are boxes that we ourselves choose, but when we die others choose our box for us -a coffin!

What then? People have different views - some say that death ends all, some think that we come back as someone else or something else, while others just do not know, but think that there *could* be life after death. This results in many fearing the unknown beyond death. God, however, makes it clear in the Bible: **"Man is destined to die once and after that to face judgement"** **(Hebrews 9:27).**

Is it possible to avoid condemnation? Yes, it is. The Bible states, **"God did not send his Son into the world to condemn the world, but to save the world through him. Whoever believes in him is not condemned, but whoever does not believe stands condemned already because he has not believed in the name of God's one and only Son"** (John 3:17,18). What now? For your security in eternity, God's answer is that belief in the Lord Jesus Christ will bring eternal life. **"God so loved the world that he gave his one and only son, that whoever believes in him shall not perish but have eternal life"** (John 3:16). Belief in the Lord Jesus Christ removes the fear of what lies beyond death.

Anon.

56

Questions in Paint

The French Post-Impressionist painter Paul Gauguin was a man of restless spirit. At the age of 17 he went to sea, but returned to Paris in 1871 where he became a successful stockbroker. By 1883 he was already exhibiting his own paintings and determined to devote himself entirely to art. He subsequently left his wife and 5 children, moving to Brittany to concentrate on painting. He then travelled to Martinique and from there to Tahiti, and then the Marquesas Islands.

Whatever his restless spirit was seeking, Paul Gauguin did not seem to find it. Prior to an unsuccessful suicide attempt he produced his famous allegorical painting entitled, *'Where do we come from? What are we? Where are we going?'* These are fundamental questions to which Gauguin did not appear to find satisfactory answers.

"Where do we come from?

The Bible is the only source available to people who want meaningful answers to such questions. To the questions 'Where do we come from?' the Bible tells us that human beings are a special creation of God; created to share intimate companionship with their creator[1]. Any explanation short of this leaves the questioner with the alternative that he or she is the product of blind chance, cast adrift in a soulless universe.

"What are we?"

The Biblical answer is that we are seekers. It tells us that God, having created humankind and dispersed them throughout the earth, wants people to seek him, reach out for him and find him.[2] For only in their creator can people find the true inner peace that seemed to elude Gauguin.

"Where are we going?"

This question is about our final destiny. The Bible is clear that there is an existence beyond this life, but presents two possibilities. The alternatives are stark and are determined by our response to the cross of Christ. **'For the message of the cross is foolishness to those who are perishing, but to us who are being saved it is the power of God.'**[3] Why is the Cross of Jesus so crucial? It's because it was there that God's Son died in your place, taking the judgement of God that was coming to you.

'Once you were alienated from God and were enemies in your minds because of your evil behaviour. But now he has reconciled you by Christ's physical body through death to present you holy in his sight, without blemish and free from accusation.'[4]

To think of the Lord Jesus' death and its significance as something foolish is to ignore God's love for you, expressed at a painful cost to Him. It is better to accept the reconciliation that God offers through the Cross, and be sure of eternal life.

Karl Smith

References are from: (1) Genesis 2:4-25 (2) Acts 17:26-28 (3) 1 Corinthians 1:18 (4) Colossians 1:21-22

57

On a Clear Line

I was feeling blue ... Needed someone to talk to ... I picked up my phone to call a friend ... No one home! I was needing advice ... someone to listen to ... just to be there ... so I picked my phone ... Busy! What can I do? Help ...! I need a clear line ... Have you ever thought about calling on God? He's always there! He's never too busy!

There are times in our lives when we face difficulties: anxiety, worry, loneliness or just feeling low. Who do you call for help, comfort, advice? Girlfriend? Family? Boyfriend? Work friend? At times like this you can so easily go through all the contacts in your phone to find somebody to talk to! But sometimes they're too busy... or they just don't understand what you're going through ... or they do - but they don't know how to help ...

What about God? How often have you called on God? And if you do, is it just as a last resort ... just another alternative? God, your Father, and your friend is only a prayer away and it's always a clear line! He's never too busy. He'll always listen and will never turn his back on you if you call on Him ... whatever the hour of the day or night. Wherever you may be, he's there with his arms outstretched, willing for you to come to Him: **"You will seek me and find me when you seek me with all your heart" (Jeremiah 29:13).**

If you need any proof that God really cares about you, think about this: He demonstrated his incredible love for you but by giving his only Son, Jesus Christ, to die for you: **"For God so loved the world that he gave his one and only Son, that whosever believes in him shall not perish but have eternal life"(John 3:16).** When Jesus suffered, it was because he was being punished for the sins of the world -that includes you! And if you'll use that clear line to God to confess your sins and to thank Jesus for dying for you, then God will forgive you completely. That's how much God loves you!

If you haven't accepted Jesus Christ as your Saviour and friend yet, why not call him now ... it's a clear line ... he will answer. **"If you confess with your mouth, 'Jesus as Lord' and believe in your heart that God raised him from the dead, you will be saved" (Romans 10:9).**

Anon.

58

Switch Off... Switch On

Imagine: suppose we used the OFF switches: what would be left? If we turned OFF our TVs, and computer games. If we stop surfing the net and watching films if we switched off the radio and Wi-Fi. If we even switched off our mobile phones, what then? Probably a lot of silence. An anxious silence, slowly filling with questions: Why am I here? Am I in a virtual world or the real world? Why don't I want to be alone? Who values me? Purpose? Meaning?

These questions still crop up - even with everything switched on. They may be harder to hear, but they are certainly there. Some are trivial. Others are important. Many are personal and others are universal. The questions are a search for Truth. Here is an answer...

Answer: I know a man who lived and died for the Truth. Here is what Jesus Christ said about his personal Truth - **"He then began to teach them that he must be killed and after three days rise again" (Mark 8:31)** And it happened. He did die and come back to life three days later. Because He said that and it happened, then the other things He said about Truth are worth looking at.

He lived the Truth: In His relationships he had integrity. In His arguments He was straight talking. And people loved Him for it **"I am the way and the truth and the life" (John 14:6).**

He spoke the truth about Himself: **"... the Son of Man did not come to be served, but to serve, and to give His life as a ransom for many" (Mark 10: 45) "Peace I leave with you; My peace I give you. I do not give to you as the world gives" (John 14: 27)**

He spoke the truth about you and me: **"For from within, out of men's hearts, come evil thoughts, sexual immorality, theft, murder, adultery, greed, envy, slander, arrogance and folly" (Mark 7: 21)**

"There is no difference, for all have sinned and fall short of the glory of God" (Romans 3:23).

You and I fall short of the best life that we can have. We are separated from God, our Creator. We can get the best by getting back to God. This means that we need to:

1. Admit we have done wrong.
2. Believe that Jesus died to take away our sins so that we can be reconciled to God.
3. Commit our lives to following Jesus to make Jesus - not ourselves - the centre of our lives.

Simple Truth. Life changing Truth. Who is at the centre of your life -you or Jesus Christ? You can "switch on": You can live the life God wants you to have when you know Him and follow His Son, Jesus Christ.

"Now this is eternal life: that they may know you, the only true God, and Jesus Christ, whom you have sent" (John 17:3).

Paul Merchant

59

Brave Fellows These

He sat down opposite me for lunch in a city restaurant. He was a Merchant Navy captain. "Talking about safety at sea," he said, "the only charity I subscribe to is the Royal National lifeboat institution - brave fellows, these I docked at Milford Haven a little time back. A storm was running high and there was no use putting to sea till it calmed down. I was sheltering near the bridge. At that moment the Mumbles' lifeboat, with his eight noble crew on board, was being turned round again to put out to sea for the second time - never to return." We reflected on the Bible verse: **"Greater love hath no one than this, that he lay down his life for his friends" (John 15:13).**

"You know, captain," I said, "there's another verse which goes even further. It says, **"God demonstrates his own love for us in this - while we were still sinners, Christ died for us" (Romans 5:8).** "I believe that through his death he saved me and, if you are willing, he can save you too."

Love in action: He has been doing his saving work for centuries. We read in the Bible that **salvation is found in no one else (Acts 4:12).** So many people are trying to get to heaven by their own efforts. Personal achievements don't cancel out sin in our lives, and the alarming, stark reality is that human souls are **"without God and without hope in the world (Ephesians 2:12).** With God to meet - sooner perhaps than we think - this might very well be a vital moment to decide. The following verses have helped me - why not you?

- **"For God so loved the world that he gave his one and only son, that whoever believes in him shall not perish but have eternal life" (John 3:16).**
- **"He himself bore our sins in his body on the tree." (1 Peter 2:24).**
- **"All the prophets testified about him (Jesus) that everyone who believes in him receives forgiveness for our sins through his name" (Acts 10:43).**

Jack Ferguson

60

The Vital Difference

One of the most famous Buddhist temples in the world is Shwe Dagon. It stands on a hill over 200 feet high and rises some 200 feet higher still. It is covered with pure gold leaf. Around its base are hundreds of small pagodas, in each of which is some relic or a teacher or Buddhism. Embedded in the solid masonry of the base is a gold box which contains some finger-bones, teeth and other parts of Buddha, who lived many centuries ago. There is another burial place in Arabia, the green mosque of Medina, under which lies the body of Mohammed. Millions of people today are his earnest followers. But, despite his greatness, he too is dead, and like Buddha, lies buried here on earth. The burial place of Confucius is a grass-covered mound in the province of Shantung, China. Confucius was also a great man and teacher, and he has influenced the lives of millions of human beings. Nevertheless he is dead, and his body too is here on the earth.

There's another tomb, cut into the rock. A tomb which had been closed with a great stone. Today, the stone is "rolled away" and the man whose body had been laid within by sorrowing friends is gone. The world-shattering truth being that, on the third day after he died, "He rose from the dead!" Yes indeed, the tomb of Jesus Christ is an empty tomb. And that's *the vital difference* between Jesus of Nazareth and all the other men who ever walked the earth. He, too, was a great preacher. He, too, was a great man. His teaching also has affected millions who believe in Him. But He was much more than a great teacher or philosopher, more than a great leader. He is the Son of God with power. That's why his tomb is empty! **"It was not possible that he should be held by death" (Acts 2:24).**

And He did not die as other men do – unwillingly. He died as a sacrifice **"for the sins of the world" (John 1:29).** For your sins and for mine. Jesus Christ, by His resurrection from the dead, has changed millions of lives. Because He conquered death and lives, all who believe in Him will live as well (John 6:40). You, too, can know his transforming life transforming power if you will receive him into your life as Saviour and Lord. The Bible declares, **"He who believes on the Son has everlasting life: and he who believes not the Son shall not see life" (John 3:36).**

H. Spencer

61

Searchers

Have you ever felt lonely? I don't mean isolation, but a feeling that no one really cares about you. You walk on a crowded street, but you feel ignored and unknown. You go to a party where friends are gathered; they're laughing and joking, and you feel left out. You feel uncomfortable because you don't fit in. Or perhaps you've supported an unpopular cause and been rejected for it. We can handle feelings of loneliness if we have a few friends or a special person whom we can talk to. If we can't speak to anyone, the problem becomes more serious. Many people search for a close friend but never find. And there are those who've experienced real friendship, but have been disappointed through unfaithfulness, or bereavement. All of us need a companion to confide in. But is there anyone who really cares?

The problem calls for someone beyond us . We don't need to search far for the person who cares: Jesus Christ. When we know Him, we need never feel unwanted or rejected again. He promised his followers, **"I will not leave you as orphans; I will come to you" (John 14:18).** He's the only one who can truly satisfy our need for friendship and love. He also said, **"If anyone loves me … my father will love him, and we will come close to him and make our home with him" (John 14:23).** Jesus is **"a friend who sticks closer than a brother" (Proverbs 18:24).**

The love of Christ for us was so great that He was prepared to die. Why did he have to die? The Bible tells us that even our best attempts to lead a good life are like **"filthy rags" (Isaiah 64:6)**. For God is just and Holy and must punish wrong. But Jesus took our punishment when he was crucified and died for us. He has done everything to restore us to a right relationship with God. He asks us to turn away from our self-centred life, and to trust that His death has removed the problem of our sin. Don't stay as one of the lonely people - still searching. God offers you his forgiveness and friendship. Why not choose Jesus Christ as your Saviour and friend today?

Anon.

62

Congestion

All over the world the traffic congestion is becoming a major problem: from Birmingham to Beijng; from Tokyo to Toronto; from New York to London, the streets of the world's great cities are choked with vehicles. Many solutions have been suggested and tried: road pricing, fuel surcharges, tolls, congestion charges and many more The problem of congested roads comes down to this: too many people travelling on the same road at the same time.

Jesus spoke about a road down which many people travel. he said, **"Broad is the road that leads to destruction, and many enter through it" (Matthew 7:13).** You would hardly think that a road leading to destruction would be such a popular highway! But Jesus was speaking in a spiritual sense. He meant that many people are leading lives that are taking them further and further from God. It is the road of pleasing themselves, with no thought for God or for the terrible cost in personal destruction. But Jesus also told us about a way to bypass the problem. There is an alternative route- one on which there are no congestion busting toll charges – and it's the way which leads to life. This way is to come to know Jesus Christ, God' Son, as your very own saviour. Jesus said, **"I am the way, and the truth, and the life. No one comes to the Father except through me" (John 14:6).**

There is no fee. There is no charge. But there is a cost - you need to turn from your own way and do a U-turn in your thinking. The Bible speaks about this change of heart and calls it 'repentance', which means to regret something and turn away from it. And the positive benefit of this repentance is that it's **"repentance that leads to life" (Acts 11:18).** Why not leave the broad road now and **"choose life"? (Deuteronomy 30:1).**

Anon.

63

Eye of the Storm

The sailing ship skips cheerfully across the sea, a strong breeze billowing it sails and every inch of canvas bursting with wind. Then the sky becomes dark. Clouds pile up. The breeze whips into a howling gale, the sea into a cauldron of foaming water, tossing enormous waves. The angry storm sucks the ship into its frenzied climax, ripping the sails and splitting the mast. Suddenly the wind dies, the heaving waves subside, a restless calm sets in. Yes - this is the eye of the storm. Just as a spinning wheel has a point in the centre that does not move, so the storm has an "eye" where all is calm. But this calm is uneasy and false. Within moments the waves renew their fury, and the ship finally capsizes, unable to resist the brutal storm pitched against it.

A very different kind of storm however, once broke out on just one man. This was a storm of hatred against Jesus Christ, God's Son. Jesus was condemned to die as the crowd shouted, **"crucify him."** Soldiers whipped him. Nails were banged through his hands and feet into a wooden cross. He was executed outside the city of Jerusalem. What a storm of hatred! Then came the eye of the storm for the Bible says, **"And sitting down, they kept watch over him there" (Matthew 27:36).** It was the false calm. Then the storm broke out again - far worse this time - for Jesus was on the cross, God punished Him - his own Son - for every sin that you and I have ever done. Relentlessly it beat upon him. Nothing held back. The storm reached its climax - then Jesus breathed his last.

"While we were still sinners, Christ died for us" (Romans 5:8). Go to the eye of the storm, gaze up at the cross, see Jesus dying there for you - and believe that **"... the son of God ... loved me and gave himself for me" (Galatians 2:20).**

Roy Dickson

64

Land of the Rising Sun

The islands of Japan are collectively known as "Land of the Rising Sun." This name is depicted on Japan's national flag, which shows a red disc on a white background, the red disc representing the rising sun. In 1945 Japan seemed anything but a country of sunrise; defeat in World War Two had left the economy in ruins, but in a relatively short time, Japan rose from the ashes of defeat to become the second most powerful economy in the world. Throughout her history Japan has been personified in the person of her emperor. Japanese tradition held that the emperor was descended from the Sun God, so that each succeeding emperor was known as, "The Son of Heaven," and believed to be divine. The last emperor to bear this title was the emperor Hirohito, but in 1947 Hirohito renounced his deity, admitting that he was human.

Israel's national flag displays a six-point star on a white background; the star is a Star of David, Israels most famous king. To Christians, Israel is the land of the great Son of David, the one of whom it is written, **"... who as to his human nature was a descendant of David ... was declared with power to be the Son of God, by his resurrection from the dead" (Romans 1:3,4).** The Son in question is Jesus of Nazareth, the true Son of Heaven. The Israel of Jesus's time was the scene of a greater miracle than Japan's post-war recovery, or any other miracle ever witnessed. The resurrection of Jesus is the most stupendous event ever recorded in human history.

Why did Jesus rise from the dead? **"He was delivered over to death for our sins and raised to life for our justification" (Romans 4:25).** Justification is when the judge declares you completely guiltless. God judged Jesus as if He had done all our sins so that He can judge those who trust Him as if they had done all the good things He did. Through faith in Jesus you can have the joy of justification for **"… if you confess with your mouth, "Jesus is Lord," and believe in your heart that God raised him from the dead, you will be saved" (Romans 10:9).** The heart of the Easter message is the message of the risen Son.

Anon.

65

Someone Cares

How are you today? This message is from someone who cares about you and is thinking about you and would like to give you some really good news. It's the best news about the best Friend you could ever have. He is a Friend who can do more for you than any other friend and His name is Jesus Christ, the Son of God. When Jesus was here on earth, he healed everyone who came to Him - He really cared about them, and the Bible says that he went about **"healing every disease and sickness among the people" (Matthew 4:23)**. Yes - every disease and sickness! Nothing was too difficult for him. He healed the bodies and the minds of everyone who came to Him, so that they would open their hearts to an even greater healing that they needed - the healing of their soul!

There were people who were cured by Him who then believed He was the Son of God. These people had their souls healed too: they went away with great joy in their hearts. But some who were healed didn't believe He was the Son of God and though their bodies were healed, their souls remained sick, they had missed the greatest healing of all - the healing of their soul. We all need this kind of healing. Many people attempt to 'clean up' or compensate for their own things in their life by doing good works, but the Bible says you need to acknowledge that you're a sinner and ask God's forgiveness. The good news is that Jesus died for your sins and rose again so that you can be forgiven and have eternal life. He is still able to save everyone who comes to him.

The Bible says, **"Whoever believes in the Son has eternal life" (John 3:36)** You can't work for it, and you can't pay for it - it's a free gift from God. The work was all done when Jesus died, and now He lives to save you when you call on Him. This could be the beginning of a new life for you. Jesus said, **"I tell you the truth, whoever hears my word and believes him who sent me has eternal life and will not be condemned; He has crossed over from death too life" (John 5:24).** So ... why not think about how much Jesus cares about you and wants to help you, then pray to him "Lord Jesus, I believe on you in my heart. Thank you for dying for me." And why not now? He will hear you and you will know in your heart that you are saved - forgiven and not condemned - and you also have a real friend for life and for eternity!

Guy Jarvie

66

Blood Donor

"Save a life today ... be a Blood Donor!"

Many of us have been blood donors at some times in our lives. Hospitals need a continuous supply to ensure their patients can survive modern operations, and to turn to full health and strength. Did you realise that Jesus, too, was a blood donor?

- You gave some of your blood, probably a pint. Jesus gave all he had.
- For you, the needle was small, sharp, and nearly painless. for Jesus, the nails were long, dull and very painful.
- For you, the chair or table was relaxing, soft and restful. For Jesus, the cross was rough and rugged.
- To you, the staff were kind and gentle. To Jesus, His accusers were mean and cruel. They spat on Him. They beat Him. They pulled the beard from His face. They put a crown of thorns on His head.
- You probably received some sweet juice, or perhaps a cup of tea, and maybe a biscuit afterwards. Jesus was given vinegar mixed with gall.
- People applaud you for your contribution. Jesus was reviled and mocked.
- Your blood has a specific type. Mine is O positive, the universal donor. the blood of Jesus is universal, positively for all.
- Your donation, at best, is temporary and may help prolong someone's life

for a little longer. His blood can save all who will accept it, forever. The Bible says that **"Without the shedding of blood there is no forgiveness of sins" (Hebrews 10:22).**

Why not accept the greatest gift someone can give, **that they down their life for a friend (John 15:13).** Jesus wants you as a friend - and he laid down his life for you.

Based on an article by Jack Smith.

67

Rescued!

A swimmer can float on water but if you cannot swim then you are a "sinker." Some time ago I went with some friends who were good swimmers to a village called Akarakumo near Lagos in Nigeria. Although I was unable to swim, I watched my friend Emmanuel and the others as they enjoyed themselves in the water. Fascinated by the rhythmical movement of arms and legs I said to myself, "I guess I could do that and enjoy myself like them" so I decided to join them. At the edge, the water reached my ankles ... as I moved further into the lagoon the level rose to my knees ... then my waist ... and then suddenly I was sinking and completely covered. But I could not float!

I struggled desperately with all my strength. I was becoming very weak ... I felt death was near, yet my friends were still enjoying themselves, unaware of my plight. All this happened within minutes, but it felt like hours. I needed help and only one person could save me. To live, I must cry for help. I took a deep breath, jumped up in the water, giving a loud shout, "Emmanuel! Help!" Then I sank again. Did Emmanuel hear me? Yes, he did. I was rescued!

What happened to me that day describes you and me! As sinners we are "sinkers", and we cannot enjoy the life which God has given us. When we attempt to do this by trying the pleasures of sin, we're only sinking deeper ... then finally, death comes, and it is too late finding God. All our efforts to rescue ourselves out of our sins are of no effect. But God in His love has provided a way to rescue us through the death of his Son, Jesus Christ.

"Everyone who believes in Him receives forgiveness of sins through his name" (Acts 10:43). But now Jesus has come alive from the dead and is able to save completely and **"Everyone who calls on the name of the Lord will be saved" (Romans 10:13).** Come to Jesus Christ in true confession of your sins and give Him that big shout - Lord Save Me!

Mark Imoukhuede

68

Lost in the Crowd?

In this day of mass movements, it is easy to overlook the individual. Sometimes it seems as though people are just cogs in a machine without any sense of personal recognition - useful while doing a job of work, but easily replaced. In one realm however, everyman is "himself." In the spiritual realm, each man has to have personal dealings with God. There is no such thing as being lost in the crowd with him. The Bible individualises us. It says: **"For all have sinned; all fall short of God's glorious standards" (Romans 3:23)** and adds: **"No one is good, not even one" (Romans 3:10).**

The point of this is there are many who will acknowledge that **"all have sinned"** who are not so willing to say, **"I have sinned."** But the Bible is quite clear. Sin is individual and carries an individual accountability. As an individual **you** were born into this world; as an individual **you** have lived your life; as an individual **you** have sinned and as an individual **you** will have to give an account of yourself to God (see Romans 14:12) **You** cannot be lost in a crowd.

"In a world of teaming millions does God really care about the individual?" you ask. Yes, he does! **"For God so loved the world that He gave His only Son, so that everyone who believes in Him, will not perish but have eternal life" (John 3:16).** God's love reaches out to the world, but response to that love is an individual thing – each one must have personal dealings with God. That God is concerned about individuals is clearly shown in the Bible, which says, **"There is joy in the presence of the angels of God when even one sinner repents" (Luke 15:10).** The Apostle Paul put it like this: **"The Son of God who loved me and gave Himself for me" (Galatians 2:20).**

Are **you** willing to face up to the word of God when it tells **you** of **your** sin? Are **you** willing to accept the fact that God loves **you**, and that Christ died in **your** place? Are **you** prepared to go further and ask the Lord Jesus Christ to save **you** from the consequences of **your** sin?

Without a doubt there are those who will laugh if **you're** serious about these matters. But bear in mind that they will not carry the consequences of **your** sin against God when **you** ultimately appear before him. **You** will, unless Christ becomes **your** personal Saviour now. Cry in your heart, **"Save me, Lord" (Matthew 14:30)** and **"O God, be merciful to me, for I am a sinner" (Luke 18:30).** Take Jesus Christ as **your** Saviour and Lord and **you** will find that salvation is a very real and personal thing
  R.V. Court

69

A Friend in Need

Morecambe in Northwest England is a wonderful place on a warm summer day, with its sands and blue sky. But there is another side to this bay, and many a walker on the sands suddenly find themselves in dire straits, held fast in unexpected quicksand, cut off by the rapidly rising tide, or hopelessly lost in the fog or darkness. It is then that a friend is badly needed, someone to come alongside and show the way to shore and safety.

In his book *Sand Pilot of Morecambe* Cedrick Robinson, the officially appointed guide to the sands, tells on how a number of occasions he was able to help those who strayed off the path into danger and who needed a friend. No doubt, as part of his work, Cedric has often risked his life to lead someone out of the danger and back to the right path. How frightening to be trapped in sinking sand with the tide coming in fast. Only someone who has lived through such an experience could describe their feelings of panic, fear and despair.

Because of life having gone wrong, is panic, fear or despair the way you are feeling right now? There is a friend who sees and understands. My friend wants to come alongside you, take your hand and lead you to safety. My friend was appointed by God to come to this world from heaven, carry a heavy wooden cross to a hill and suffer there a lonely, fearsome, forsaken death. It was something He came to do for each one of us, taking the punishment for the sins we had done. God accepted His sacrifice and raised Him from the dead to be a living saviour and guide to all who call upon Him. My friend is Jesus. He is very near to you right now, near enough for you to call out and be heard. Gods promise to all those who turn by faith to Jesus is: **"Everyone who calls on the name of the Lord will be saved" (Romans 10:13).** This is written for all who feel they have lost the path through life, who are lonely, in despair and who need a friend.

Anon.

70

Jack's Story – A New Song to Sing

I was born in 1908 in Cumbria, England. I was christened and confirmed as a boy, and I sang in the church choir. I left school at 14 and began to work on a farm. I loved horses and my farm work, and I loved music and dancing. I had no worries in the world. This lasted for about 10 years. Then I started to think about life. There were things in it that were not as they should be. When I was 25, I moved to another farm to get a better wage. One day I heard that a worker was coming who was a preacher. I did not like the idea of working with a preacher. However he turned out to be a decent sort of man. He read his Bible and prayed every day. I began to think about my sins. We had many conversations together. Because I was christened and confirmed I thought I was alright with God. My preacher friend quoted to me from the Bible that I must be "born again" and that I was not alright.

One night in December 1934, I realised that I had to make a decision. I decided to come to the Lord, just as I was. As the hymn says, I heard the voice of Jesus say, "Come to me and rest, lay down thou weary one, lay down thy head upon my breast." That night my friend and I knelt down together, and I gave my life to the Lord: "I came to Jesus as I was - weary and worn and sad; I found in Him a resting place and He has made me glad" I was very happy. As I followed the plough the Lord put a new song into my heart. Now years later, much has changed on the farm. The horses have gone, but I still have the joy that the

Lord put into my heart that day when I discovered that Jesus is the Son of God, who loved me and gave Himself for me (Galatians 2:20). Perhaps there is something missing in your life. Here are some words of Jesus for you to think about:

"I tell you the truth, no one can see the Kingdom of God unless he is born again" (John 3:3).

"I tell you the truth, whoever hears my word and believes him who sent me has eternal life and will not be condemned; for he has crossed over from death to life" (John 5:24).

Jack Hunter

71

Problems & Solutions

Do you have any problems in your life? Who doesn't? We all have problems to deal with, and each day seems to add a new one to the pile. Can you relate to any of these? Problems with my marriage or relationship? Problems with my children or other family members? Problem with debt or my finances? Problems with feelings of guilt? Some or all of these can fill our minds until we can't think of anything else.

What better solutions do we have to make things better and happier for ourselves? Sometimes the problems of life seem overwhelming, and we feel we have no one to turn to. Nevertheless when we close our eyes and say, "Please, will someone help me?" I can assure you there is someone listening. In the Bible, when Jesus says **"Come to me all you who are weary and heavy laden and I will give you rest" (Matthew 11:28)** He is inviting you to get to know Him so, when we pray to God, He is always ready to listen. He loves you so much that He wants to help you and relieve you of your heavy burdens so that you can have peace in your heart.

Our biggest problem is that we have turned our backs on God. We live in a world full of problems caused over many centuries by people's selfishness, hurtful attitudes and rebellion against all that is good. Each of us adds to the world's problems and their own by doing things we know to be wrong. That rejection of God makes us feel he is a million miles away, even though **"He is actually not far from each one of us"** (Acts 17:27).

God cannot ignore sins and justice must be done - His judgement has to be carried out. Thankfully however, when we see only the problem, God has the solution: **"For God so loved the world that he gave his one and only Son, that whoever believes in Him shall not perish but have eternal life"** (John 3:16).

"Whoever" of course includes you, so if you believe this good news, thanking God for sending his son to die to deal with your sins, you will be saved! What a wonderful gift! Once the main problem of your sin is dealt with, the air will be clear between you and God. You will know he is listening to your prayers, and he will give you strength for the difficult times as well as the good ones. I can tell you this from experience. Whatever help you need, God has the answer. All you have to do is ask - He will help you find the way.

Anon.

72

"I'll Be Back!"

Just a few hours before the Lord Jesus was crucified, He gave his followers this promise: **"Let not your hearts be troubled. Believe in God; believe also in me. In my Father's house are many rooms. If it were not so, would I have told you that I go to prepare a place for you? And if I go and prepare a place for you, I will come again and will take you to myself that where I am you may be also" (John 14:1–3).**

He did go back to heaven; this is witnessed in Acts 1:9–11. Not only did his disciples see him go, until a cloud received him out of their sight, but the angels immediately confirmed the promise of the Lord Jesus, **"This Jesus, who was taken up from you into heaven, will come in the same way as you saw him go into heaven" (Acts 1:11).**

Further details of His coming again are given by the Apostle Paul, who became a Christian sometime after the Lord Jesus had returned to heaven. He wrote comforting words to the Christians in Thessalonica, who were very anxious to know about the return of Jesus because some of them had died. Paul assured them that Jesus's is promise held good for all Christian believers, whether alive or dead. He wrote: **"For this we declare to you by a word from the Lord, that we who are alive, who are left until the coming of the Lord, will not precede those who have fallen asleep" (1 Thessalonians 4:15).**

The Bible answers the questions Jesus's followers have asked through the years. Let's look at some of them:

- Will he come himself or will he send someone else for us? **"The Lord himself will descend from heaven" (1 Thessalonians 4: 16-17).** He said, **"I will come again" (John 14:1-3).** The angels said, **"This Jesus... will come in the same way" (Acts 1:11).** It is to be a personal return by the Lord for his own.
- How will he come? He will come to the air, with a shout, with the voice of the archangel and with the trumpet call of God (1 Thessalonians 4:16-17).
- Will believers alive on earth at the time of his coming have any advantage over the dead in Christ? No, **"The dead in Christ will rise first. Then we who are alive, who are left, will be caught up together with them in the clouds to meet the Lord in the air..." (1 Thessalonians 4:16-17).**
- Will it be for all time? Yes, the word of God says so: **"so we will always be with the Lord" (1 Thessalonians 4:16-17).**
- When will he return? We are not given any date; it could be at any time.
- What will happen to our body when Jesus returns? We shall all be changed. Our bodies will be transformed, the change being affected in a moment of time, in the twinkling of an eye (1 Corinthians 15:51-52). **"When he appears we shall be like him, because we shall see him as he is" (1 John 3:2).**

Jesus is coming again - no doubt about it. Are you ready for his coming? **HAVE YOU ACCEPTED JESUS AS YOUR SAVIOUR?**

Neville Coomer

73

While the World Slept...

Great events attract great crowds. Royalty, local officials and newspaper reporters claimed their privileged seats while the rest of the people linger outside locked gates and secure fences. Everyone wants to be there and see what is happening and to share the excitement. The greatest event in the history of the world took place about 2000 years ago in a small town in a Roman occupied province in Israel.

The small town of Bethlehem was quiet that night and this great event - the birth of a boy - took place in a stable because the inn was full. But only Mary, the child's mother, and Joseph her husband knew what was special about the new-born infant. They had been told, **"You are to give him the name Jesus, because he will save his people from their sins," and, "He will be great and will be called the Son of the Most High" (Matthew 1:18 – 2:12).** The important local people knew nothing about it. It was shepherds out on the hillside who were the first to hear the good news. the message came to them, **"Today in the town of David a Saviour has been born to you; He is Christ the Lord" (Luke 1:26-38). "Suddenly a great company of angels appeared, praising God and saying, 'Glory to God in the highest, and on earth peace to men on whom his favour rests'" (Luke 2:1-20).**

Mary and Joseph did receive visitors that night; ordinary shepherds who were the first to see God's salvation and who returned to the hills glorifying and praising God for what they had seen. But that wasn't all. God had told the important news to wise men in a distant country. they came bearing gifts and asking for the infant king because, **"We saw his star in the east and have come to worship him."** Israel's King Herod knew nothing about it and when he did find out, his only thought was to eliminate his rival.

The effect of that great event is still being felt today, as men, women and children around the world believe in that baby who, when He was grown up, died for their sins. The Bible says about Jesus, **"For God was pleased to have all his fullness dwelling in him, and through him to reconcile himself to all things ... by making peace through his blood, shed on the cross" (Colossians 1:19-20).**

Jesus was born for you. Don't be like Herod who tried to exclude Jesus from his life. Instead, thank God for a Saviour, Jesus Christ, who died for you on the cross. God wants to hear your prayer of gratitude for His Son who suffered in order to bring peace between God and you. **"Thanks be to God for his indescribable gift!" (2 Corinthians 9:15).**

David Webster

74

What Have I To Do With Jesus?

There once was a man who lived in a graveyard. He was mad, of course. He was a terror to the local inhabitants and had been put in chains more than once. but he seemed abnormally strong and always broke loose. Had he existed quietly, it might not have been too bad for others. You can imagine the effects of his screaming and shouting day and night, and of his appearance bathed in the blood of his self-inflicted wounds.

One day, the Bible tells us, this man met Jesus, the Son of God, and he was never the same man again. He saw Jesus coming in the direction of his graveyard and he ran at Him. Instead of attacking Him, however, or attempting to terrify Him, he crumpled up at His feet and cried out: **"What have I to do with you Jesus, Son of the Most High God?" (Mark 5:1-20).** There are many people today who ask the same question. As you read this, the Son of God, the Saviour of the world, is being presented to you. Are you saying in your mind, "What have I to do with you, Jesus?"

The answer is that you have very much to do with the Lord Jesus Christ and he has very much to do with you. You have no reason to fear him. He loves you and offers to save you from your "graveyard" of unbelief and godlessness. You are sane, and God has given you the common sense to be able to choose or reject right or wrong (Deuteronomy 30:19). Will you allow the Lord Jesus to overcome all that opposes Him in your life? He has the power to do this, and to save you completely, if you will come to God the Father by Him (Hebrews 7:25).

He is waiting to give you peace in your heart; joy and love in your life; and a life forever in the ages to come. What have you to do with Jesus Christ? Receive Him into your heart by faith today.

"As many as received Him, to them He gave the power to become the sons of God, even to them that believe on His name" (John 1:12).

"For God so loved the world that He gave His only begotten Son, that whoever believe within Him should not perish, but have everlasting life" (John 3:16).

Graham Cox

75

Let's Face the Music and ...?

Let's Face the Music and Dance is a well-known popular song written in 1936 by Irving Berlin for the film *Follow the Fleet.* It featured a dance duet with Fred Astaire and Ginger Rogers. *'Face the music'* is what we say when we have to confront something difficult. Have you ever wondered where the phrase originated? One popular account relates to music hall artistes going on to the stage and having to face the pit orchestra – and the audience of course. If the performance wasn't appreciated, audiences could become quite hostile! A more sobering explanation is the sombre 'music' of the drum roll which announced a military execution.

Music generates a wide range of emotions and is one of life's pleasures. Most brass bands have hymns in their repertoire. One classic – *'Eternal Father strong to save'* has all the atmosphere of danger at sea and the confidence of God's protection. Another is *'Abide With Me'* with its words of comfort at the thought of life ending.

There are more than 185 songs in the Bible: The first is by Moses when the Israelites escaped across the Red Sea and Pharaoh's army was destroyed by the returning water.[1] King Solomon wrote over 1000 songs,[2] but the greatest of these is the beautiful story of love told in the *Song of Solomon*.[3]

The Lord Jesus Christ sang with His disciples before leaving Jerusalem to go to the Garden of Gethsemane.[4] In the space of a few hours he was arrested, tortured, humiliated, then executed. **His crucifixion was the culmination of God's great plan for our redemption.**

We have a greater danger to face than that of the hostile audiences at the theatre mentioned at the start: one day we will have to face our Maker – God, and He will judge what we have done with our lives. We deserve punishment, but the Lord Jesus faced up to this for us so that we could escape it. The purpose of Christ's death is explained in the popular Easter hymn, *'There is a green hill ...'* One verse reads: *There was no other good enough to pay the price of sin. He only could unlock the gate of heaven and let us in.*

In Revelation – the last book of the Bible – there is a rousing finale to its collection of songs. We read: **'And they were singing the song of Moses, the servant of God, and the song of the Lamb: Great and marvellous are your works, O Lord God, the Almighty, Just and true are your ways, O king of the nations.'[5]** Why not accept the work of the Lord Jesus dying to save you from the penalty of sin today, and be assured of joining the joy of that great song in Heaven – NOT *'facing the music'* of eternal judgement for your sins.
   Anon.

References are from: (1) Exodus 15:1-18; (2) 1 Kings 4:32; (3) Song of Songs 1:1; (4) Matthew 26:30; (5) Revelation 15:3

76

"I'm Lost"

Is there life after death? Is life a waste? Any meaning ... any hope? "I am confused"... "I'm in a maze"... "I'm lost" But there is good news - where from? The Middle East. When? 2000 years ago. Who from? A Carpenter! Yes, 2000 years ago a Carpenter in Israel said, **"The Son of Man came to seek and to save what was lost" (Luke 19:10).** So if you say, "I'm lost", you need not be because this carpenter came to seek and to save you. "Oh, if only I could believe that!" That Carpenter was Jesus Christ who also said, **"Come to me all you who are weary, and I will give you rest" (Matthew 11:28).** Jesus came to rescue you from everlasting separation from God. He came to give you meaning, purpose and hope in your life. if you take him as your personal Saviour, the promise is **"I will never leave you; I will never abandon you"** (Hebrews 13:5). So... **"If you confess with your mouth, 'Jesus is Lord' and believe in your heart that God raised him from the dead, you will be saved"** (Romans 10:9) ... and never be lost again!

Anon.

77

Have You Heard the One About?

An old comedian used to do a joke about a glazier who insisted on fixing 164 of his friends' windows until he realised his need - to fix a crack in his glasses. The old ones are the best, eh? That one's 2000 years old. The original version (told by the Lord Jesus) is much more surreal. It's about a man who tries to tease a tiny speck of dust out of his brother's eye but can't see very well to do it because he's got a dirty great plank of wood sticking out of his own eye. We can all be like that. We are all very good at setting the world to rights- but unless we set to right ourselves, it's all rather pointless. Never mind what's wrong with other people, what about you? What about me?

A lot of things in our lives are really other people's fault, but even making the most generous allowances for that, sooner or later we all have to face up to one big fact: the buck stops with me. I've got to take the responsibility for what I myself have done wrong in my life, the times I have gone against what I know to be right, the times I have hurt others. And so have you. The Bible says: **"If we say we have no sin, we deceive ourselves, and the truth is not in us ... (Matthew 7:3-5)** And it has a point, doesn't it? Thankfully it continues: **"if we confess our sins, he is faithful and just to forgive us our sins and to cleanse us from all our unrighteousness" (1 John 1:8-9).**

How can God forgive you and give you a clean record? Because the Lord Jesus himself took the punishment for your sins when He died on the cross. That's how much it matters and that's how much He loves you. If you are honest with God right now and admit you're a sinner, trusting what the Lord Jesus did was enough to save you from His anger, you will be saved from it and begin a new, changed life with Him.

Anon.

78

Birthday

Your personal, special day, once a year- your birthday! The day of gifts and greeting cards received from friends and relatives; perhaps a celebration and a special meal; children are excited before their birthdays - looking forward to party; for adults it can be the time to reflect on one more year past and to consider the year ahead. Whether we like it or not, our birthday reminds us of how old we are! If we are in the 'older' range, we may prefer to forget! My date of birth is 22nd August 1975. 1975? What does that mean? It tells me it is one thousand nine hundred and seventy-five years from ... the time when a certain person was here on this earth - Jesus Christ. Every time we mention any year in our calendar, we refer to the time that Jesus Christ lived. He spent 33 years of his life showing us the character of God. He came to this earth with a task to do - a voluntary task that took him into the depths of sorrow and pain. He died a cruel death by crucifixion. When He died, he suffered for our sins. The Bible says, **"He was delivered over to death for our sins" (Romans 4:25);** He died to take away our guilt before God so that we can be forgiven: **"God did not send his Son into the world to condemn the world, but to save the world through him" (John 3:17).** So, **"Whoever believes in the Son has eternal life ..." (John 3:36).** When you thank Jesus for dying for you, you are saved from God's judgement. You are born again to eternal life. Then you will have a 'birthday' to celebrate forever! (Anon.)

79

McCaig's Town

As one of Scotland's premier tourist towns, Oban is overlooked by a Roman Colosseum-type monument. Viewed from the harbour, it forms a very impressive sight as it is silhouetted against the sky. But what is it? It is a permanent monument to big-hearted local banker - John Stuart McCaig - who had a care for the town's people. McCaig had decided to assist the local unemployed stonemason's by employing them to build a monument that would be a permanent asset and benefit to the area. The Tower, begun in 1897, was to house a museum and a statue of the philanthropist. McCaig had good plans but his untimely death in 1900 meant that the source of finance dried up and although he left money to further his project, the will was set aside by a court action brought by his surviving sister. There was no one willing to complete the building. The tower sadly became known far and wide as McCaig's Folly. The locals do not like that title because McCaig intended to do good, and it's now known as McCaig's Tower.

The story of this tower is a reminder of the story Jesus told regarding a man who planned to build a tower but did not sit down, plan properly and count the cost (Luke 14:28-30). None of us can see what lies ahead and neither can we tell when our days will be over. What will we leave behind? A life that has the reputation of a folly or something that will commend us for what we have achieved? In this parable Jesus implies that we are foolish if we do not plan ahead. The surest thing in our life is death. Have you planned for that?

How can we know and plan? The Bible says that if we die in our sins then we cannot be in heaven and our life work will be a folly (John 8:21-24). It doesn't need to be like that. Jesus said that he didn't come to call the righteous, but sinners (Matthew 9:13). To realise we are sinners is necessary, and to be fit for heaven we need to prepare. Are you prepared? You need to repent (be sorry for your sins) and accept Jesus as your Saviour. To rescue you from hell cost Jesus his life on Calvary's cross, and he completed the task - no folly there! Accept his free salvation today and you will be prepared and leave no regret or folly behind you.

Anon.

80

One Minute to Midnight?

It has often been said that as far as mankind is concerned the clock is at *one minute to midnight!* Ecologists now see that it is almost too late to repair the damage we have done to our world. Population explosions come with the attendant horrors of disease and starvation. The natural disasters seem to arrive more and more often. Nationalism and "ethnic cleansing" stalk the globe, and there is still the threat of "weapons of mass destruction" caused whether from the thousands of nuclear missiles and chemical and biological agents still held by nations across the world, or from those held by so-called "rogue states." Life is very uncertain. Time is certainly running out.

Is there a solution to the problem? Must it always be a case that **"the courage of many people will falter because of the fearful fate they see coming upon the earth" (Luke 21:26).** If only we looked to man, then the answer must be yes. We have failed, and everyday our televisions and newspapers emphasise how we have lost our way. However, there is a wonderful alternative for those who are prepared to look. If you only stop pursuing the time worn and hopeless course of looking to improve yourself from within. instead you need to be like those who **"set their hope in God" (Psalm 78:7).** For despite world unrest, He has not abdicated His authority; He is still in complete control. Not only God's power, but also His love is made available to anyone who will admit that they are powerless to help themselves. That love is summed up

in "For God so loved the world that he gave his only Son, so that everyone who believes in him will not perish, but have eternal live" (John 3:16).

The most dramatic event in anyone's life is when they turn from themselves, admit that they are sorry for what they have done in the past, and accept that only Jesus Christ can help them live a better life. Do this right now, and you need have no more fear of what the future will bring, for your life will be in the loving hands of the one who holds, and is, the future.

Based on a tract by A. Hall.

81

Which Way Now?

Finding your way round a town can sometimes be quite a problem, especially when it's crowded. You can always follow the crowd of course - but that way you would probably miss something you particularly wish to see. What you need is a plan of the town to see where you are going. Finding your way through life is much the same. You can follow the crowd and do as everyone else does, but that is no guarantee that the way most take is the right way. Jesus had some advice about following crowds: **"For wide is the gate and broad is the road that leads to destruction, and many enter through it. But small is the gate and narrow the road that leads to life, and only a few find it" (Matthew 7:13,14).** IIow can we find a way? We need a plan. The Bible is God's plan to guide us through life and show us the way. What is this way? Jesus said: **"I am the way and the truth and the life. no one comes to the father except through me" (John 14:6).** The eternal Son of God came to earth as a man, Jesus of Nazareth, and lived among men for about 30 years, showing men the kindness and goodness of God. At the end of that time he was put to death by crucifixion, not simply because the authorities were against him, but because in our sinfulness we had strayed away from God: **"We all, like sheep, have gone astray, each of us has turned to his own way" (Isaiah 53:6).** A loving God has provided a way back to himself, through Jesus Christ: **"For God so loved the world that he gave his one and only Son, that whoever believes in him shall not perish but have eternal life" (John 3:16). (Anon.)**

82

The Truth About Life

Modern medical science achieves wonders. It has enabled doctors to prolong human life and keep people breathing even after they have suffered extensive damage to their bodies. People have been resuscitated when breathing had recently stopped. Hearts which have ceased to beat have been re-started and kept going by means of intricate machines. But once a person is medically dead no human effort can restore life. God alone can give life for the Bible says **"He Himself giveth to all life, and breath, and all things"** (Acts 17:25).

I was saddened recently when I visited a hospital where a young woman who has no arms or legs, and cannot hear, speak or see, lies motionless 24 hours a day. She cannot communicate and no one knows her thoughts, but she has life of a kind. In great contrast, the millionaire tours the world in luxury enjoying every pleasure which takes his fancy. For some people life consists of boredom, worry, fear, sickness or poverty. For others it is pleasure, prosperity and plenty. However, for the majority of people it is an average, uninteresting, routine existence. Is this the whole of life? Has it not more to offer? Surely it has, for Jesus Christ said **"I am come that they may have life, and may have it abundantly" (John 10:10)** Jesus contended that the great purpose of life is to find God through Him, to love Him and serve Him. Only then shall we experience the abundant life which Christ came to give.

Certain people who died recently left instructions for their bodies to be put into "deep freeze," preserved intact, until medical science advances sufficiently to bring them back to life. Their hopes are centred in science, in the ability of men, but they are doomed to disappointment. They will come back to life, for the Lord Jesus Christ said, **"Marvel not at this; for the hour cometh, in which all that are in the tombs shall hear His voice, and shall come forth ..." (John 5:28).** The Bible also says **"It is appointed unto men once to die and after this cometh judgment" (Hebrews 9:27).**

When Jesus Christ said **"He that believeth [on me] hath everlasting life"** (John 6:47) what could He have meant? He allowed many of His followers to suffer martyrdom and early death, so He could not have been speaking about avoiding natural death. Further, He taught that all persons continue to exist after death, so if some have eternal life it cannot mean merely existence after death. No, it is more than that. Eternal life is offered as a free gift in Jesus and it carries the absolute assurance of never-ending life with Him. The Bible makes it clear that the death of the Lord Jesus Christ is the basis for this gift. Repentance before God because of our sin and faith in Christ that He died to put away our sin, is the way this blessing comes to us. If you want God's salvation there is no alternative to faith in Christ (Romans 6:23).

Anon.

83

Two Bestsellers

In March 1852 the book 'Uncle Tom's Cabin' was published in the U.S.A. It was to exert an extraordinary influence on thousands of readers and on the future of America itself. In due course it became famous and was translated into more than 20 languages. It was an exciting, moving story, full of unforgettable real-life characters. But it was much more than that — it rapidly became a 'best seller' because it also contained a great message. This message was a passionate attack on slavery in America. The terrible picture it painted of slavery in a civilised country could not be ignored because it was based on fact. The book also brought home forcibly the feelings and the conviction that had been growing steadily for some — which was that slavery was wrong and unworthy of a great nation which had grown up in a struggle for freedom.

Such ideas met with resistance from the rich slaveowner planters and this led eventually to the American Civil War. President Lincoln, who was ultimately to emerge victorious as the champion of the slaves, said in a famous address at a victory rally: "Our fathers brought forth on this continent a new nation conceived in liberty and dedicated to the proposition that all men are created equal ... We here highly resolve that this nation under God shall have a NEW BIRTH OF FREEDOM ..." Lincoln's final victory brought not only an end to war but also an end to slavery. How the slaves rejoiced at what must have seemed to them the greatest news in the world. The message of Uncle Tom's Cabin had been effective and America had its new birth of freedom, the emancipation of all its slaves!

Another best seller is the Bible. It also contains a vital message for it is God's word to us. Today, all the world over many people can testify to the fact that it has completely changed their lives. The Bible's life-giving message is based on the fact that God's own Son, Jesus Christ, died to save and free us from sin. This must surely be the greatest message in the world as we consider our condition before a Holy God.

"For all have sinned and fall short of the glory of God" (Romans 3:23). The Bible makes it clear that we are all slaves to sin. But our position is not hopeless because the victorious Son of God died on the cross for us and three days later rose again from the dead. The belief that 'Christ died for *me*" will bring the peace of forgiveness and also freedom from sin's penalty — the judgement of God in the life after death.

Paul described the gospel message as **"The power of God for salvation to everyone that believes" (Romans 1:16).** Paul also lived in a day when slavery was commonplace — but he knew the delivering power of the gospel, a power that liberated slaves to sin and gave to them a new birth of freedom. This new birth brings us into God's family and also assures us of God's power in our lives to help us combat sin from day to day.

In Washington, America, there is a monument erected to the memory of Lincoln. At his feet crouches a grateful, liberated slave. The monument was erected by funds solely contributed by freed slaves; they gave because they loved the memory of their saviour and friend — it was their way of showing their appreciation. Have you shown your appreciation to the Lord Jesus Christ for giving His life to free you? If not, please consider this opportunity for doing so now and believe in Him.

Anon.

84

Above All Else - The Incomparable Christ

Around 2,000 years ago there was a Man born contrary to the laws of life. This Man lived in poverty and was reared in obscurity. He did not travel extensively. Only once did He cross the boundary of the country in which He lived; that was during His exile in childhood. He possessed neither wealth nor influence. His relatives were inconspicuous, and had neither training nor formal education. In infancy He startled a king; in childhood He puzzled intellectuals; in manhood He ruled the course of nature, walked upon the waves as if pavements, and hushed the sea to sleep. He healed the multitudes without medicine and made no charge for His service.

He never wrote a book, and yet all the libraries of the country could not hold the books that have been written about Him. He never wrote a song, and yet He has furnished the theme for more songs than all the songwriters combined. He never founded a college, but all the schools put together cannot boast of having as many students. He never marshalled an army, nor drafted a soldier, nor fired a gun; and yet no leader ever had more volunteers who have, under His orders, made more rebels stack arms and surrender without a shot fired. He never practised psychiatry, and yet He has healed more broken hearts than all the doctors far and near.

Once each week the wheels of commerce cease their turning and multitudes wend their way to worshipping assemblies to pay homage and respect to Him. The names of the past proud statesmen of Greece and Rome have come and gone. The names of the past scientists, philosophers, and theologians have come and gone; but the name of this Man abounds more and more. Though time has spread nineteen hundred years between the people of this generation and the scene of His crucifixion, yet He still lives. Herod could not destroy Him, and the grave could not hold Him. He stands forth upon the highest pinnacle of heavenly glory, proclaimed of God, acknowledged by angels, and feared by demons, as the living, personal Christ, our Lord and Saviour.

We are either going to be forever with Him, or forever without Him. It was the incomparable Christ who said:

"Come to me, all you who are weary and burdened, and I will give you rest"
(Matthew 11:28).

"Whoever comes to me I will never drive away. For I have come down from heaven not to do my will but do the will of him who sent me. And this is the will of him who sent me, that everyone who looks to the Son and believes in him shall have eternal life, and I will raise him up at the last day" (John 6:37-40).

"Do not let your hearts be troubled. Trust in God, trust also in me" (John 14:1).

Anon.

85

The Decision That Changed My Life

I was born in Vienna in 1927 where my Jewish father and Catholic mother brought me up in a rather carefree atmosphere. On reaching my teens I was old enough to understand that political unrest was beginning to change the face of Europe. I well remember the radio broadcast of the Austrian Anschluss in 1938 and the Munich crisis after which, like many others, I fled my native country. I joined my brother in England and soon we became fully integrated into the British way of life. Though I had been brought up in the Jewish tradition, this merely entailed attending synagogue on Saturdays and learning Hebrew. At school I was excused prayers because of my religion and this practice continued even after my father died in 1940. During all this time I had no thoughts about a personal involvement with God, though I sometimes asked this impersonal Being for favours I desperately wanted. It was not until I reached my 18th birthday and took up work in Northern Ireland that I heard of such a thing as a personal relationship with Jesus Christ. That possibility was brought before me as I listened to the Gospel preacher at a baptismal service in a local church. Afterwards the pastor and his wife took me into their home and explained the Gospel fully so that I had a "head" knowledge of God's salvation and forgiveness long before I had any desire to experience it personally. I continued to attend such meetings on occasions and, when any appeal was made for repentance and faith in Christ, I longed to know more about this but something always prevented my own acceptance. Then it happened. During a quiet prayer meeting the longing for that personal assurance of Jesus Christ as my Saviour became very real to me. I went home and in prayer told God that I accepted the Lord Jesus Christ as my personal Saviour. I realised that I faced the judgement of God because 1 was a sinner and the only way to escape this was to trust in the Saviour He had provided. It was difficult even then to put my experience into words but I went to bed that night and for the first time in my life knew with certainty that I had peace with God. No flash of lightning, so to speak, no voice from the sky told me that I had been saved, but what I had read and heard from the Bible assured me.

It soon became easy for me to tell others and I even joined in outdoor testimony meetings. As a result of my public witness I was forced to leave my job; however, I was more than compensated (see Philippians 3:7-9) through meeting another like-minded Christian, saved only a month after me. Soon we were married and started our life together in the joy of this new-found faith. The decision that changed my life was the beginning of a new life for me (see 2 Corinthians 5:17) and I can testify today, 35 years on, that peace with God through our Lord Jesus Christ has remained continuously with me. Looking back on my life, I recall that the Bible verse **"the heart is deceitful above all things, and desperately wicked" (Jeremiah 17:9)** was the first eyeopener to me and caused me to think about my sinful position before God. Other Bible verses such as the following, which prior to that time I never knew existed, helped to give me the assurance that God's salvation was in Jesus Christ alone: **"He [Jesus] was pierced for our trangressions, He was crushed for our iniquities; the punishment that brought us peace was upon Him, and by His wounds we are healed" (Isaiah 53:5).** Now I pray that all who read this short story of the most important event of my life will accept Jesus Christ as their Saviour and know with me, and millions of others, the peace with God and complete happiness in life which it brings (Romans 8:28).

Inge Woods (nee Herzenberg)

86

Love's Greatest Monument

The Taj Mahal is the jewel of Indian architecture. It was built by an Indian emperor, Shah Jehan, in memory of, and as a burying place for, his favourite wife. Even after 300 years the Taj is as beautiful as when it was built - with white marble inlaid with precious stones. It was a monument to love — the love of a rich man for his wife.

The love of Shah Jehan was love for the woman who loved him, but there is a far greater love than that — it is the love of God for us who have sinned against Him by going our own way. The Bible says: **"This is love; not that we loved God, but that He loved us, and sent His Son as an atoning sacrifice for our sins" (1 John 4:10).** And again — **"God demonstrates His own love for us, in this: While we were still sinners, Christ died for us" (Romans 5:8).**

Many who have visited India have gazed in admiration at the beauty of the Taj; and some would be moved by the love of the man who built such a monument in memory of his wife. But millions the world over, as well as in India, have marvelled at the love of God in sending His Son to die for their sins. With deep thankfulness they have accepted Jesus Christ as Saviour and made Him Lord in their lives. They have read His words: **"God so loved the world, that He gave His one and only son, that whoever believes in Him shall not perish but have eternal life" (John 3:16).**

Have you responded to that love? Have you said, like the Prodigal Son when He returned to his father, **"Father, I have sinned against heaven (against God) and in thy sight"? (Luke 15:21).** Whenever he said that, he found the father's arms around him in love. We are all prodigals![1] We have all sinned against the God who loves the God who sent His Son to die for us. The cross of Christ is the greatest monument to love — God's love and our sin. Respond to that love today, gladly accept Jesus as Saviour and make Him Lord in your life.

Those who die unforgiven meet the judgement of the One whose love they despised, Jesus Christ who died for them and rose again from the dead to be their Saviour. He is alive and is waiting for you to call upon Him. The Bible says: **"Everyone who calls upon the Name of the Lord will be saved" (Romans 10:13).** Please read these verses in the Bible today, and receive Christ by trusting in Him. He waits to save you and when He does it is for time and for eternity.

    Anon.

---

[1]   spending money or resources freely and recklessly; wastefully extravagant:

87

What Can You Believe Anymore?

We've learned to laugh at everything, turned it all into a joke. Most of what we watch or listen to is people making fun of other people, telling you not to trust anything, being smart at somebody else's expense. You can make fun of everything. War, love, sex, death, family, everything can look silly. The trouble may be that we're so busy laughing that we haven't left anything to believe in. You know the kind of person I'm talking about, like Hawkeye in *Mash.* He gives the same treatment to everything and everybody. He's usually brighter than average and sometimes you envy the quickness of his satire. But now, when you think about it, you realize that there's nothing left to believe in.

If war is funny and marriage is hilarious, if business is rotten and love is lust, and if God is somebody that we made up when we were very young and innocent, then we're living in a particularly hopeless world. You're all alone like a fly in a spider web. Sometimes it feels like that. Somebody has done a good job of telling us to make fun of everything; somebody who is so unhappy that they don't ever want us to be happy.

God says that He is in charge of everything and that He knows what is happening. The sad voice says that it is all happening by accident. God says that, in the middle of all the rebellion and indifference, His will is being carried out. The sad voice says that fate is terrible to us and that nothing can be trusted. Remember this - God sent His Son to prove beyond any doubt that He can be trusted. He came to prove that God has the answers to all the things we do not have answers for, like weakness and loneliness, hatred and destruction, disaster and pain, sin and death ... especially death. God knows all about these things because He allowed Jesus to die a cruel death, having done nothing wrong, totally alone.

I should have died because I have done wrong, but Jesus suffered instead. Now I am forgiven - and He gives joy. Joy, remember? "Don't be afraid. I bring you good news of great joy ... a Saviour has been born to you."[1] It's for real, and you can have it too! There is somebody to trust. If we are ever going to get the message of joy into all the unhappy faces, then God needs people who will trust Him, to switch off the sad voices that say "You can't believe anything," and start living for Christ. The old, tired world may be disillusioned and short on trust, but God is looking for those who are ready to break away into the experience of eternal life. "I tell you the truth," Jesus said. "Whoever hears my word and believes Him who sent Me has eternal life and will not be condemned; He has crossed over from death to life. "[2]

   Anon.

Bible Quotes: 1. Luke 2:10-11; 2. John 5:24

88

What Would You Have Done?

He was a farmer and a very wealthy man. Everything he touched seemed to turn to gold. Year after year he had bumper crops. And one year the harvest was so big he just did not have room to stack it all away. Complete reorganization was called for. That was obvious. Quickly he decided for larger and more modern buildings. Money talks, they say. Certainly there were plenty of men in the trade ready to do the job for him with the minimum of delay. It was a one-man show. He had no partner, nor did he need one. He had all that it takes. Plenty of business acumen. All his plans were made and the future seemed rosy indeed. "You have plenty laid up for many years," he said to himself. "Time to ease off a bit now, and have a good time. Eat, drink, and be merry," Familiar words, for lots of people talk the same way today. The three things men live for were all included:

- Plenty of goods - that's treasure.
- Take your ease - that's leisure.
- Eat, drink, and be merry - that's pleasure.

Let's face it, life is made up of these three things for many. But the more we get the more we want. For these things have a way of never really bringing satisfaction. And they have an uncanny knack of fading away just when we think we have got hold of them. It was so with the farmer. He was settling down to really enjoy himself, when suddenly tragedy struck. A heart attack and the man was gone - and the irony of it was that it happened the very night that his plans were finally made.

He made some awful mistakes, of course. Providing for his body, he forgot about his soul. God in heaven made his crops grow, but he forgot that, too. He took all God's gifts but never had a thought for the Giver — at least, not until his dying moments, but then it was too late. Yes, too late then. He had lived for the present only. Reckoning on time, he had forgotten eternity. A foolish man, God called him, and he was indeed, for this life is so short and the next so long. But it was all so attractive, the huge profits and the luxuries they brought. He could think of nothing else — not time to think anyway. He lived for himself, and life was happy — until that fearful night.

Friend, in similar circumstances, what would you have done? The Lord Jesus Christ said (for the story of the farmer is His, basically, not mine), **"A man's life consisteth not in the, abundance of the things which he possesseth."** It is true and it's worth thinking about. True, abundant life is found in Jesus Christ alone, by God's grace, through faith.

Alan Toms

89

Is It Too Late?

Too late for what? Well, to make the world a better place. Most of us have a feeling that it is. The idea that the world was bound to become better through education and social reform was a kind of dream many had. But the advent of weapons of mass destruction and the increase in crime and violence have shattered that dream. In his last book, *'Mind at the End of its Tether* (1945), H. G. Wells wrote, "There is no way out, or round, or through ... The stars in their courses have turned against him (man). Fate closes in more and more swiftly upon mankind." Many feel like Wells about it. We know how crime and lawlessness are increasing.

Is it too late for God to help us? No, it is not. He will yet make this earth a more delightful place than the philosophers have ever dreamed of. Would you like to read about it? You can, in the Bible. Read Isaiah 2:1-4; 11: 1-9; 32:17,18; 35:1,2 and Revelation 20:1-6. But before those good days come, there will be days of great trial and sorrow on the earth. You can read of this in Matthew 24:21,22 and Revelation 6:14-17. Best of all, it is not too late for you to be saved, and to get right with God, If you do, then you will certainly see the good days that God will give this world, and you wall not come into the days of judgement.

"How can I get right with God?" you may ask. If you live in a land where there are many Bibles, you may have heard how Jesus died on the Cross for sinners. Many Christians are continually urging others to believe on the Lord Jesus and so be saved. That is what we need - we need salvation from our sin. It was for our salvation that Jesus died and rose again. That was marvellous love! The Bible says, **"Herein is love, not that we loved God, but that He loved us, and sent His Son to be the propitiation for our sins" (1 John 4:10).**

Definitely, it is not too late for you to be saved — JUST NOW! But make it NOW. Do not put it off, for even tomorrow may be too late for you. A well- known hymn says, "Tomorrow's sun may never rise, To bless thy long deluded sight; This is the time! Oh then, be wise! Thou wouldst be saved — Why not tonight?" Think of Jesus dying on the Cross, and then say in your heart — AND HE DIED FOR ME. When you trust Him, and are saved, then tell someone else that it is not too late for them to be saved.

Anon.

90

Bill's Question

Every British soldier was at his post in the trenches. The grim death-roll of the 1914-18 war was still steadily mounting. The barrage of shells was getting heavier and heavier when suddenly there was a terrific explosion over the heads of the soldiers, and within moments Bill lay dying. His mates, realizing that he was mortally wounded, did all they could to ease his pain. Bill's closest friend noticed that with difficulty he was trying to speak, and bending his head to catch his last words was surprised to hear Bill ask the question, ''Does anybody know the way to heaven?'' The exploding shells of heavy artillery could not have made a greater impact. "The way to heaven!" Bill's question was passed faithfully along the line, "Bill's dying and wants to know the way to heaven."

But each time the question brought the same reply. Nobody knew. Crawling amidst the flying shrapnel his friend called out, "Bill's dying and he wants to know the way to heaven. Can anyone tell him?" Still there was no response. Then, one of the battalion anxious to help shouted that he might get the answer from Charlie who was at his machine-gun post along the line. Bill's friend was now almost beside himself with anxiety. It was a grim race against time.

"Charlie," he gasped, "Bill's been hit and is dying fast. Can you tell him the way to heaven?" "Yes, I can," replied Charlie, "but you know that under battle orders none of us is allowed to leave his post; take this little New Testament, and I'll underline the few words you need to read to him - then Bill will know the way to heaven," Bill's mate was overjoyed, and grasping the New Testament he scrambled back to his post and bending over his dying friend read, with great feeling, the words that Charlie had underlined, **"For God so loved the world, that He gave His only begotten Son, that whosoever believeth on Him should not perish, but have eternal life" (John 3:16).**

Bill was quiet for a few moments, then, gathering his waning strength he opened wide his arms and gasped, "Thank God its 'whosoever'" and within seconds he was gone. All this made a tremendous impression upon Bill's friend, and he was determined that every man he had questioned should now know the answer to this all-important question. The open New Testament was passed from man to man, then back to its owner, that the message Charlie had underlined should be read by all.

My friend, perhaps Bill's question fits your own case. Are you clear about this matter? The Lord Jesus said, "I am the way ... no one cometh unto the Father, but by Me" (John 14:6). There are many ways that seem right to men, but God tells us that the end of these is death (Proverbs 14:12). When Bill put his faith in Christ his name was written in heaven, for Jesus Himself said, "Rejoice that your names are written in heaven" (Luke 10:20). Can you?

Harold Caldwell

91

Know Any Loopholes?

Readers' Digest recently told about a man who did not have long to live. He asked a friend to bring him a Bible. On returning with the Book his friend expressed surprise that he should want a Bible in view of his past evil and immoral life. "I want to see if there are any loopholes" was his reply.

Many people are secretly fearful that they might be facing the judgment of God in the life to come, but for various reasons most manage to keep the prospect as nothing more than a remote possibility. We fool ourselves with the idea that we will not be much worse off than others and probably fare better than most. Also that God may not exist at all and, if He does exist, surely He will be loving and forgiving.

The *Readers' Digest* also carried an anecdote in which a minister said "Nearly everyone is in favour of going to heaven but too many are hoping they'll live long enough to see an easing of the entrance requirements." Many like to think that there is a heaven to which they will hopefully go, but as to any certainty of admission that is quite another matter. They argue that the Hitlers and the Mafia of this world will surely be turned away but average decent living people must have a good chance of being received.

"Is there a definite answer to this uncertainty and if so what chance do I have of finding it" you may ask? There are numerous denominations and often they give varying answers. Books and leaflets on the subject are countless and more often than not they disagree. If you feel confused I understand, for so did I until I turned to the Bible and found God's forgiveness. In this matter we must be guided by the Bible alone. If you are seriously interested in finding God, knowing His forgiveness and having the assurance that you will escape His judgment in the life after death, then hear for yourself what the Bible says.

This message preached in Bible times by the followers of Jesus is the same message we now send you. Hear the words of the disciple Peter: **"Jesus of Nazareth ... went about doing good and healing ... for God was with Him. And we are witnesses who ate and drank with Him after he rose from the dead and He commanded us to preach to the people and to testify that He is the One ordained by God to be judge of the living and the dead . .. that everyone who *believes in Him* receives forgiveness of sins through His name"** (Acts 10:38-43).

You are not saved by believing the historical facts about Jesus. You must realise that your sin, that is all the wrong things you have done, brings God's judgment upon you. The only way to forgiveness is to believe that it was for you personally, for your sins, that Jesus Christ suffered and died. Do not reject God's salvation. He loves you and is calling men everywhere to receive Christ as Saviour. Thousands the world over are responding to this message. Why not you?

Anon.

92

You Cannot Hide

A famous national leader once said, "You can run but you cannot hide" - it was a warning international terrorists. Sadly, in many countries there are people running away to escape punishment. As we look around, people seem to be running in many directions. Some are travelling through life constantly running to achieve their ambitions. Others travel the world to see new sights and experience different cultures. Some rush to fill their lives with pleasure. Others run to drugs or drink to compensate for life's boredom.

Do you know where you are running to? Will you find peace and true happiness when you get there? There is a well-known man in the Bible called Jonah who was swallowed by a fish. There must be millions of people who know about Jonah but who do not know the whole story. Jonah was trying to run away from God when he was swallowed by the fish and at the end found that he had to face God. The incident can be summed up by the old song: *"O sinner man, where will you run to, O sinner man, where will you run to, O sinner man, where will you run to, All on that day?"* Jonah is like many people who are avoiding and running away from God but who do not realise that God cannot be avoided. The Bible makes clear that God will find you even if you go down into the earth or rise up into the heavens: **"If I go up to the heavens, you are there; if I make my bed in the depths, you are there" (Psalm 139:8).**

Probably you have never thought of yourself as running away from God. But every time you ignore Him, every time you reject Him, and every time you disbelieve Him you are running away from Him. If you are running away from God, where are you running to? Who are you running to? Are you running away from God or are you running towards Him in order to find Him?

When you choose to run towards Christ you hear His words about Himself. Whoever listens to Him is listening to God. Whoever believes in Him is believing in God. Jesus Christ brings you forgiveness when you stop running from God and decide to put your trust in Him. He brings you peace and happiness which is lasting and does not depend upon the fleeting pleasures of life. He brings you the assurance of eternal life now and in the life after death. Jesus Christ said, **"I give them eternal life, and they shall never perish"** **(John 10:28)** and **"Do not let your hearts be troubled. Trust in God; trust also in me ... I am the way and the truth and the life. No-one comes to the Father except through me" (John 14:1-6).**

Please do not try to avoid or run away from God. The only way to meet Him, having the assurance of eternal life, is to repent and trust in His Son, Jesus Christ, who died for you. Then there will be no need to run and hide.

Anon.

93

The Good Samaritan

The Red Cross, a charitable organisation which has saved the lives of thousands, is well known throughout the world. It was founded in the early 1860s to care for wounded soldiers of all nationalities. Today the Red Cross helps in all kinds of disasters, not just in wars. It all started about 1859 when a young banker, Henri Dunant from Switzerland was travelling in Italy on July 24th and he saw the battle of Solferino. After fifteen hours of fierce fighting some 40,000 soldiers lay dead or dying. There was no one to help them. Seeing the plight of the wounded he got local women and girls to take the soldiers, whatever their nationality, to any suitable buildings which they then used as temporary hospitals. Soon he was known as "THE SAMARITAN OF SOLFERINO."

He later wrote a book about these experiences and by 1863 a committee of 5 had started the Red Cross in Geneva with a membership of 16 countries. Today, this wonderful world-wide organisation does its best to save people's lives and it works in both peacetime and wartime covering all parts of the world.

Nearly 2,000 years ago Jesus Christ spoke about "first aid" when He told that now famous story popularly entitled "the Good Samaritan." The story tells about a traveller who was mugged, robbed and left half dead. Help was not offered by passers-by who should have cared, but by a complete stranger "the Good Samaritan." He gave immediate "first aid" and without asking for payment took care of the poor unfortunate victim. In a sense that is just like the Red Cross- give help where help is needed.

In God's eyes all people of all nationalities are in real need because they are sinners. Jesus gave Himself upon the cross and, in a sense, because of His death some would call it a "red cross." Why did He die? The Bible tells us that He died to save men from the penalty of their sins. So we all need a "good Samaritan" — we need a saviour who is Jesus Christ. By trusting in Him, make His saving death your certain assurance of God's salvation for eternity.

Think about these Bible quotes:

- **"Therefore He (Jesus) is able to save completely those who come to God through Him" (Hebrews 7:25).**
- **"God demonstrates His own love for us in this: While we were still sinners, Christ died for us" (Romans 5:8).**
- **"This righteousness from God comes through faith in Jesus Christ to all who believe" (Romans 3:22)**
- **"Whoever believes in Him [Jesus] is not condemned, But whoever does not believe stands condemned already because he has not believed in the name of God's one and only Son" (John 3:18).**

Anon.

94

My Moment of Glory

Bill Kazmier from Arizona, U.S.A was the world's strongest man. He came top in a "strong man" contest against other international supermen, and in a TV interview after the event he said, "I am the strongest man who ever lived." His feats of strength included bending thick iron bars, pulling a twelve wheel truck along a road and lifting the equivalent of six heavy men. In another event he won during the six-day contest he lifted a massive tree trunk above his head and threw it away; he then gave a victory sign. Asked by a reporter why he gave it, he replied, "Just to enjoy my moment of glory."

Most of the competitors punish their bodies with such amazing feats of strength that they reckon they could be dead by the time they are forty years old. Then some will exchange their few moments of glory for an eternity of . ... what? Most of us will never be as famous as Bill Kazmier but in a sense we all enjoy our moments of "glory." They seem to make life worthwhile — a word of appreciation, an admiring glance or a loving touch. How they each boost our ego. But when life is over, what then?

When we are young life lies ahead of us and seems to offer such a long existence, but soon we discover that the years rush by. Looking back in older years life seems so short. The Bible describes it as being like a puff of smoke which appears for a few moments and then quickly fades away. It would be meaningless and sad if that was all there was to man's existence. Thankfully God also tells us in the Bible of life beyond death and holds out the assurance for you to have eternal life with Him through faith in Jesus Christ,

Think about these Bible quotes — To those who believed in Him Jesus said:

"If I go and prepare a place for you, I will come back and take you to be with me that you may also be where I am" (John 14:3-4).

"Whoever believes in Him [Jesus] is not condemned, but whoever does not believe stands condemned" (John 3:18).

God also warns of judgement to come for those who reject His gift of free salvation and forgiveness through faith in Jesus Christ. **"Serve the living and true God, and . . . wait for His Son from heaven, whom He raised from the dead — Jesus, who rescues us from the coming wrath" (1 Thessalonians 1:9-11).**

If you reject God in this life can you blame Him for rejecting you in eternity? Sin is the root cause of our failure to respond to God's love and while we are not responsible for being born as sinners, we are responsible if we do not trust in Jesus Christ as our Saviour when we get the chance.

This could be your chance! So what are you doing with it? Trust is not difficult if you know that the person you are trusting will never let you down - Jesus said **"Whoever comes to me I will never drive away"** and when they come to Him says, **"I give them eternal life and they will never perish."** Bill Kazmier was not always the strongest man in the world but Jesus Christ will always be the only one who is able to bring you God's salvation. The Bible says **"Salvation is found in no one else ... for there is no other name by which we must be saved" (Acts 4:12).**
    Anon.

95

It Was For Me

After the Great War of 1914-1918, the late Duke of Windsor - who was then the Prince of Wales - was on a visit to one of the many hospitals for the war-wounded. Passing from ward to ward the Prince was deeply moved to see so much suffering in men who once were the flower of British manhood but were now shattered and maimed for life. Stopping to chat with those who were able, he sought to encourage and cheer the men as they lay in bed. Near the end of his visit, he enquired if there were any patients whom he had not seen. Conferring among themselves, the hospital authorities replied, 'There is yet one, but we would rather you did not see him, for your own sake.' With his usual quiet but firm manner the Prince responded, "I will see him.' In a side ward lay a patient, blind and with marred face, and with neither arms nor legs.

For a moment the Prince stood, apparently horrified and shocked. On regaining his control, he bent down and with tears in his eyes he kissed the disfigured face of the patient. Through his tears he said, "IT WAS FOR ME.' Let us think of another sufferer ~ Jesus Christ, the Son of God. The Bible says of Him that His face was so marred more than any man, and His form more than the sons of men (Isaiah 52:14). As to His suffering we read, '**See if there be any sorrow like unto My sorrow.'** The holy Son of God was marred and bruised by the savage beatings that He received from the Roman soldiers who had been ordered to beat Him. And then, with nail-pierced hands and feet, Jesus bore the ultimate of hatred and physical torture that they could inflict. But that was not all, for the Bible says that He bore our sins in His body on the tree. He was crucified — FOR WHOM?

Consider your place in this verse from the Bible (Isaiah 53:5): **"He was pierced for .... transgressions, He was crushed for .... iniquities. The chastisement of .... peace was upon Him; And with His stripes .... healed."**

Will you put your name there today, and thank Him for doing it all for you? Surely the love of Christ is proved by His dying for you. Surely this will touch your heart, and cause you to seek God's salvation so dearly bought for you by the Son of God. Yes, you can be saved, and know that you are saved, by placing your faith in the Man of Calvary. Take Him as your Saviour and Lord now, and one day soon you will see Him in Heaven, still bearing the marks of His suffering for you.

It was for me, yes all for me,
O love of God, so great, so free;
O wondrous love I'll shout and sing,
He died for me, my Lord and King.
(John M. Whyte)

John McGlinchey

96

More Beyond

Towards the close of the fifteenth century the pillars of Hercules were stamped upon the coins of Spain, and underneath was written the legend, 'Ne plus ultra '— ' Nothing beyond.' The inscription was altered by the discovery of America. When Columbus set foot on the shores of the great land that was never to bear his name it was decided to delete the 'ne' and leave the other two words standing, " Plus ultra '— 'More beyond'!"

Yes, friend, there's more beyond, there's another life beyond this. The Bible says so and it has never been proved wrong. Jesus said in Mark 10:30 that those who follow Him will receive "*in the world to come* eternal life." Yes, the world to come. Sobering thought! Again the Bible is clear as to how we shall all reach that world. It is by what Paul describes in Acts 24:15 as the resurrection "both of the just and unjust." But in the resurrection the just and the unjust will not live together or work together any more as now they do. For in the world to come there is what the Saviour termed, "a great gulf fixed" between them. Fixed, friend, fixed for all eternity. Serious business this; that's why God made us write, publish and now hand you this.

The devil will tell you that it is not serious—but God has known the craftiness of the devil since the day he first sinned and God says that he is a deceiver. He is a wise man who says with Paul, the Apostle, " For I believe God." They tell us that when the great ship Titanic sank on its maiden voyage to America, the scene outside the White Star office in Liverpool beggared description. A great crowd of the relatives of those who had taken passage on that ill-fated vessel thronged the street and all traffic was suspended. On either side of the main entrance a large board had been placed. Above one was printed in large letters, ' KNOWN TO BE SAVED' and above the other, 'KNOWN TO BE LOST.'

Every now and then a man would appear from the office bearing a large pile of cards on each of which was the name of one of the passengers. As he stood at the entrance and faced the crowd and held up the name, a deathly stillness swept over that great congregation as it watched breathlessly to see in which direction he would turn and to which of the boards he would pin that name, either on the side of the *saved* or *the host.* There was no blackboard for those who were *neither lost nor saved.'*

Friend, God has warned us plainly that we come into the world all in one class. But our attitude to the Bible and to the great God and Saviour of whom it speaks sorts us out into one or other of two classes. They are called in the Bible "the just and the unjust" or "the saved and the lost." And all you have to do to be lost is simply to do nothing about it. But if you wish to be saved you must come to Christ for eternal life in a definite act of believing and commitment.

Yes, the trouble is defiling sin in our very nature and being. I have it—you have it. You may shut your eyes to it, gloss over it, or do what you like with it. God simply says, "All have sinned"—and that settles it, for He is the God whom we have to answer to.

A young man, very ill in a city infirmary said to me last night, " I am too scientific to believe that." Friend, there's no time to speak like that. The motto found inscribed in an old Chinese garden read, "Enjoy yourself, it is later than you think!" Yes, later than you think. Do not believe the devil's lies about the Bible. Famous scientists and naturalists have been among its most devout believers. Whatever you do believe God about sin, for it will separate you for ever from Him if it is not cleansed and forgiven before you die.

Take, for example, the wonderful verse in 1 John 1:7 - **"and the blood of Jesus His Son cleanseth us from all sin."** That is one of God's promises. You can rely on it—it will never fail. Today there are men, women and children of all grades of society entering into peace through resting on God's promise. It is not a matter of effort on our part, but rather of rest. The work was all on God's part, <u>the one and only basis for God forgiving a sinner is the death of His Son on Calvary.</u> Friend, believe that and be saved from the wrath to come. Then, looking to life's remaining days, say:

> " Were the whole realm of nature mine,
> That were an offering far too small;
> Love so amazing, so divine.
> Demands my heart, my life, my all."
> (Isaac Watts)

Jack Ferguson

97

Ruin to Restoration

My mother was born on the Milton Lockhart Estate in the Clyde valley, Scotland, where her father was head gardener from around 1920 to 1950. She recalls her father caring for the garden and grounds around "The Big House." Recently she visited her birthplace and all that was left of the gardener's cottage was an ivy-covered wall and a pile of rubble. The site of "The Big House" was covered with weeds and nettles.

During the nineteen seventies and eighties, the house had fallen into disrepair however, in 1987 a wealthy Japanese actor name Tsugawa saw its potential and bought the tumbledown remains for £800,000! Then he had it dismantled stone by stone and transported via the Trans-Siberian Railway to Japan where the mansion was eventually rebuilt and restored to its former glory!

Milton Lockhart House had been a lost cause; no-one in Scotland had been willing to invest in its restoration. It needed someone who was rich and willing to save it from ruin. Did you know you are in a similar situation to that? The Bible describes you and me as a lost cause. It says we are **"conceived in sin"**[1], born with a self-choosing nature, inherited from our ancestor Adam. It says that **"all of us have sinned and fall short of the glory of God"**[2]. God can't just pretend our sins never happened, because He is fair and just. The Bible also says we are **"dead through our trespasses and sins,"**[3] and so we are unable to save ourselves. And no other human being can save us either, not even the wealthiest – **"for the redemption of the soul is costly and must be let alone forever."**[4] What we need is someone who sees our potential, who has substantial means and has much more power than us to rebuild our lives and save us from eternal ruin.

My mother remembers a stone plaque on the wall of Milton Lockhart House. On it was carved the crucifixion scene – a reminder that Jesus the Son of God endured the cross to take away our sins. Like that Japanese millionaire, He **"came to see and to save that which was lost,"**[5] but He paid such a high price. God didn't just ignore our sins. Instead, He punished His Son as though He had committed your sins and mine. Now all you are required to do is trust God that this alone is enough to save you, and in your heart and mind ask Him to save you personally. He's waiting to make you completely new.

Anon.

References are from: (1) Psalm 51:5 (2) Romans 3:23 (3) Ephesians 2:1 (4) Psalm 48:9 (5) Luke 19:10

98

Borrowed Crib

"Cribs" is a popular American MTV show in which celebrities give a guided tour of their lavish homes. However, appearances can be very deceptive: it was reported that certain celebrities had **borrowed a property from someone else** and passed it off as their own! When Jesus, the Son of God came to earth from the throne of Heaven, as a baby he was laid in a manger – *a borrowed crib!*

More than once as an adult Jesus "slept rough." He said, **"Foxes have holes and birds of the air have nests, but the Son of Man has nowhere to lay his head."**[1] and even when he died, his body was laid in a *borrowed tomb.*

Celebrities may impress us with their wealth, but Jesus came to earth to impress us with God's love: **"...though he was rich [in heaven], yet for your sakes he became poor, so that you through his poverty might become rich."**[2]

On many occasions he had compassion on others and went out of his way to help people. In spite of his wonderful miracles (the evidence of his Deity) **"He was despised and rejected by men..."**[3] Men crowned him with thorns instead of gold. They mocked, scourged, and nailed him to a wooden cross. Yet, even on the cross he prayed, **"Father, forgive them..."**[4]

Why? The answer is found in his own words: **"The Son of Man [Jesus] came to seek and to save that which was lost."**[5] By dying on the cross, Jesus the Son of God made it possible for lost sinners like us to a) have their sins forgiven and b) to find their way back to God because **"God laid on him the iniquity of us all."**[6] To those who put their trust in him, Jesus says: **"In my Father's house are many rooms ... I am going there to prepare a place for you."**[7]

So if you receive Jesus by faith today, you can be confident that, when your life here is over, he will receive you into your own wonderful "crib" in heaven.

> *Upon a life I did not live,*
> *Upon a death I did not die;*
> *Another's life, another's death,*
> *I stake my whole eternity.*
> (H. Bonar)

Anon.

References are from: (1) Matthew 8:20 (2) 2 Corinthians 8:9 (3) Isaiah 53:3 (4) Luke 23:34 (5) Luke 19:10 (6) Isaiah 53:6 (7) John 14:2

99

Peace of Mind

I was 21 years of age and living away from home. It was during many months of isolation in Iceland that I had time for serious thought and recognised that something was missing in my life. Often I found myself thinking about God, the Bible, and the need to prepare for life after death. But my beliefs were hazy, and I lacked any certainty. I knew there must be a God and I believed in a historical Jesus, but it made no difference to my life. I felt the need to put my life right with God, so I decided to join a church. My hopes were high the day I took part in a service which initiated me into full membership of my national church. I thought, "this is the day that will change my life — now I will be a new person!"

Soon I was disillusioned with formal religion. Far from being a new person, I still had doubts and uncertainties. I visited other churches and read more books, but life was the same as before. I married, changed my employment, changed my house but there was no real change in me. Once more I was aware that the certainty and peace I so much needed was eluding me and it continued so for nine more years. I needed Christ and there was no one on hand to lead me to Him. As a sinner I stood condemned and did not know it.

By now I was 30 years old and for the first time in my life a verse out of the Bible challenged me: **"If any man be in Christ he is a new creature."** So, it was possible to get a fresh start, to become a new person, and the possibility was held out to "any man." But what did it mean to be "in Christ"? I sought out a friend who could help me and learned for the first time the real reason for Christ's death. I learned that despite my so-called respectable life, I was a sinner in God's reckoning for the Bible says, **"all have sinned"** (INSERT VERSE). When Christ died He bore the punishment that my sins deserved, and by believing in Him I was accepting His sacrifice on my behalf.

This acceptance of Christ as my own Saviour had been missing in all the instruction I had ever received. Now I saw it all I trusted Jesus Christ and thanked God for sending Him to die for me and an inward peace came into my heart such as I had never known before. I saw that the basis of God's salvation was not anything I had done, or could do, but rather what Jesus Christ had done on my behalf. If you are searching for true peace in your life you will find it the same way as I did, in Jesus Christ.

Anon.

100

Where Will You Spend Eternity?

We live in momentous times. Our fast-changing world is accelerating towards the destiny God has planned. For this reason, you must make a decision about your eternal future. 2000 years ago Jesus came to die for the sins of the world, but each individual must make a proactive choice to accept or reject God's way of salvation - that Christ died on the cross for your own sins. To do nothing is to reject God's salvation and will mean that your eternal destiny will be in hell and the lake of fire. Meanwhile the Bible tells us that, in God's precise timing, notable events will unfold: Integration between the European nations will continue to evolve. Born-again Christians will suddenly disappear when Jesus comes and takes them to heaven. A man whom the Bible calls the Anti-Christ and "the Beast" will be given power to rule this world for 7 years during which time there will be unparalleled suffering! No-one will be able to buy or sell unless they take the mark of the beast. After those 7 years, Jesus will return to earth to reign as King of Kings for 1000 years. Why choose to go through the most terrible suffering there has ever been on this earth, and after that to end up in the lake of fire, when God has already provided the way of escape by sending Jesus to die for your sins on the cross? God commands you to repent, turn away from your sins and place your trust in Jesus Christ for eternal salvation. Will you accept Christ or reject Him? Your decision determines your eternal destiny!

John Peddie

101

Epilogue

You have been reading many illustrations from 100 writers. They have one clear message: **"Christ died for our sins, according to the scriptures"** (1 Corinthians 15:3). You may ask "Why?" Those who trust in Jesus are able to say, **"The Son of God loved me and gave Himself for me"** (Galatians 2:20). May you know this blessing! Please now read God's word - the Bible - a little each day.

Neville

About Hayes Press

Hayes Press (www.hayespress.org) is a registered charity in the United Kingdom, whose primary mission is to disseminate the Word of God, mainly through literature. It is one of the largest distributors of gospel tracts and leaflets in the United Kingdom, with over 100 titles and many thousands dispatched annually. In addition to paperbacks and eBooks, Hayes Press also publishes Plus Eagles' Wings, a fun and educational Bible magazine for children, and Golden Bells, a popular daily Bible reading calendar in wall or desk formats.

Also by Neville Coomer

At the Cross: 100 Personal Testimonies of God's Grace in Christ

Since 1985, Neville has gathered stories from different men and women about their 'encounter' with God that resulted in personal salvation. By making these testimonies available, our prayer is that some might come to know Christ as their very own Saviour, and those that already belong to Him will be encouraged to tell again and again the great things God has done for them.

Life's Experiences: 100 Stories of God's Power, Presence and Purposes

This collection of true stories from people of all ages and from all walks of life in different countries around the world reminds us of something very important indeed - whether it's the big things or the small things in life, God and His Word, the Bible, have proven time and again to be reliable, faithful and deserving of our complete trust!

Reflections on the Greatness of God

This book was produced as the result of a kind gesture from someone in Northern Ireland who sent me a bookmark with Psalm 46:10 and the words "BE STILL AND KNOW THAT I AM GOD." I decided to do just that! TO BE STILL - I found that very hard. Doing it daily, it became easier. It was not difficult to fill my mind with "The Greatness of God." I invited a wide variety of people to pen their thoughts on that subject. They have done so, willingly. As you read these beautiful thoughts, may your minds be illumined to know and appreciate God.

Bible Prophecy Panoramic Chart

This panoramic prophecy chart book illustrates God's purposes through the ages, as revealed in the Bible. Each page of the book features a panel from Jo Johnson's hand-painted chart. Alongside each panel are detailed Bible quotes showing how God's purposes of love towards the human race have unfolded. The final pages dramatically illustrate the final showdown between the Antichrist and God.